# *Shhhh*
# DON'T TALK ABOUT THAT!

*A Childs Journey & How Spirit Unleashed My Potential*

GAIL WEBSTER CHT

Copyright 2020 by Gail A Webster

Cover and Illustrations by Michelle Casal

All rights reserved. This book or any portion thereof may not be Reproduced or used in any manner whatsoever without the express written permission of the publisher except for the use of brief quotations in a book review.

Printed in the United States of America

First Printing, December 2020

ISBN: 978-1-7357019-0-5

Independently Published

www.gailwebster.com

www.mindmysteries.com

# Dedication

**This book is dedicated to my mother Marie**

She never gave up on me, my children, or any family member. She was my mother, my cheerleader and survival teacher. Her last months of life she would say if I ever wrote a book people would not believe it. I said do not worry Mom I will write one. She smiled I miss her every day. What went from do not talk about that to handing out my business cards. Life is about love and living. It took a lot for me to get this photo. She died 6 weeks later. Be your best authentic self.

My mother Marie my biggest cheerleader in life even though I drove her crazy with worry with all my free-spirited warrior energy antics.

My father Gerry a fun-loving kindhearted man who just never really grew up.

My grandparents Alice and Winfield who I spent a lot of time with.

All my wonderful friends, there are too many to name who stood by me with all the ups and downs of my journey.

My beautiful sister Liz, mother -in- law Dora, my children Levi & Sean, my nephew Jason

My time employed by the DOD. It kept me from welfare and out of poverty while raising two boys as a single mother. My adventures over sea's and the many military friends I made along the way. My outstanding civil service tenure.

My ex-boss Steve Hamill with the DOD who made my life so miserable that I created my own business doing what I love by helping others.

The company I contract with who has the platform that has allowed me to sharpen and grow my skills over the years.

My psychic friend Brenda Hanna who has been there for me since my oldest son was 4 and who fostered me with love, support, and encouragement to be me no matter what others thought. The one who really understood me.

The many teachers that I have learned from and there have been many.

To the many I will connect with in the future

# Table of Contents

**Chapter 1:** Is this real or is this just my imagination? ........3

**Chapter 2:** Deja Vu: My life as an empath ........13

**Chapter 3:** Lightning Calling ........24

**Chapter 4:** Old Souls, New souls, and Connections ........31

**Chapter 5:** Empathic Impressions ........39

**Chapter 6:** The Trance – Tuning In and Out ........49

**Chapter 7:** Saturn Returns ........58

**Chapter 8:** Just Knowing ........66

**Chapter 9:** The Dragonfly ........74

**Chapter 10:** 2020 Vision ........82

**Chapter 11:** Vibrational Destination ........89

About Edgar Cayce ........93

**Chapter 12:** We are all Connected ........98

**About the Author** ........108

**Resources** ........110

# Acknowledgements

There is so much more to our mind and imagination than we could ever comprehend. In this compelling book, Gail pulls back the curtain and gives us a glimpse behind the scenes of the intuitive world and teaches us how we may live a more harmonious life as we learn to pay attention to our sensitivities which are always guiding us and protecting us.

Victoria M. Gallagher

Hypnotist and Best-Selling Author

Practical Law of Attraction

"Shhh... Don't Talk About That!" is a gorgeous masterpiece that takes you by the hand to your most gorgeous self. So get ready to honor who you really are and visit the sacred and hidden realms of your perfection.

Shelley Stockwell-Nicholas, PhD

President of the International Hypnosis Federation

Author "Spiritual Counselor's Secrets"

This is a delightful autobiography of a well-known medium. It begins with her developing her psychic abilities as a young child and fine-tuning them as an adult. This book is a real page turner as she describes how her abilities saved her life at times. As an empath she found it difficult to wear second-hand clothing as she would pick up negative vibrations from the previous owner. This is a must read for anyone interested in psychic phenomenon. I found it difficult to put down once I started reading it, you will too.

Devin Knight

# Chapter 1

## Is this real or is this just my imagination?

*The intuitive mind is a sacred gift and the rational mind is a faithful servant. We have created a society that honors the servant and has forgotten the gift.*
*Albert Einstein*

Have you ever been told "Oh that is just your imagination" when you saw something as a child? Have you ever heard something that just came out of nowhere, and you asked the person next to you and they said they did not say anything? How about getting a whiff of a scent when that item is nowhere near you? Or what about that feeling you get when it feels like you have been somewhere before, but you know you have never been there? I love it when you think about someone, and they call or just show up. If you are finding yourself in these situations with these inescapable feelings, then you have found the right book, or the book has found you.

As far back as I can remember, back when I was just a young girl, I had a very high level of sensitivity and intensity. I also remember being told how I was not to pay attention to these thoughts, feelings, and emotions. Not because I feared them, but because others did. I learned this all the long, hard way, but then again it was my path to walk so that I may share my experiences and insights with you. If you have ever questioned what you saw, felt, or just knew without knowing you knew, I truly understand. My hope and intention is that this book will give you some much needed answers.

I will begin the story with how I progressed and grew. How you can tune in yourselves without feeling weird or strange. We are all born feeling and we are all connected to our higher selves and, if we listen, we can tune in with amazing results. Not everyone will discover how it works for them the same way I did as we are all individuals. Just like we all have a fingerprint that is unique to us, our body, mind, and spirit are too. I will illustrate how it worked for me; you may find similar events but that it has your own individual imprint. Let yourself tune in as you read the journey, and how I was able to grow and fine tune my abilities with doing the work. Some of us are just destined to do this work and I am one of them. In astrology, if you know where your north node is placed, it will show your soul's purpose. Now, did I know this logically before I had an astrologer explain that to me? No, yet I always had that urge that I could not shake.

My purpose here in this lifetime is to study shadow work. Now some of you may get creeped out by that statement, but please let me explain what that means to me: To study that which is not seen by the naked eye but can be "felt" through other senses. Have you ever had a small child ask you about someone that they see but you cannot? How about your pet staring at something, barking at the invisible? I have a memory like an elephant, even back to infant times. As an infant, my mother claimed all she could see in my crib were my big, gorgeous eyes. Even at that young age I was already showing sensitivities to the world around me. I even had to be fed a special baby formula as breast feeding had become unpopular in the late 50's. My connection with cats began at that age as well. My first cat was named Jojo. He was a cross eyed, crooked tailed Siamese cat that slept with me in my crib. He used to enjoy riding in the car with us. I was devastated and cried myself to sleep rocking the crib when he was stolen out of our car. This went on for weeks. My mother did everything she could to console me, but that cat and I were connected.

JoJo tried to come home to us, but we moved soon after and the move started the grief all over again for me. I was between 2-3 years old. I just knew he would not find us, and I was sad.

It was in this new apartment when I started talking about seeing people. Then the sleepwalking started, and the dreams. I woke my parents up all the time. My father knew how much I loved music and how much I loved to dance so he would take me to this little diner around where we lived to have something to eat. While there, we would sit at the counter and he would put me up on the counter as he played Chubby Checker and the twist on the jukebox. That is where I really started to become a performer in the making.    I am a dancer. I love moving my body to music. Music calms, soothes, motivates, and hypnotizes. People, of course, loved it, I was little and had it down pat. My dad thought if he wore me out that I would sleep better at night. That did not stop the dreams or sleep walking. I fell down the stairs one night and really hurt myself sleep walking. I went over the railing and landed on one of those old metal heating radiators. That is when my mother said this apartment is dangerous and wanted to move again, and we did.

Sleepwalking, also known as somnambulism, is a behavioral disorder that originates during deep sleep and results in walking or performing other complex behaviors while asleep. It is much more common in children than adults and is more likely to occur if a person is sleep deprived. Now I was sleep deprived because of the visits and dreams. We moved to White Court, I remember that street name. It was at this apartment that my mother installed the hook & eye lock towards the top of the door so at night she could lock it and it was out of reach. Can you imagine your 3-year-old wandering down the street in the middle of the night? I did that once. Scared my mother to death.

My fondest memories of my father were here. I remember sitting on the lime green sofa in the living room watching TV with my father and he would laugh hysterically at several shows. Of course, I would laugh with him, laughing is contagious. These are the shows the Red Skelton, Ed Sullivan, Jackie Gleeson, and Lucy. Now some of you may know what I am talking about or others may say "who?" Luckily, we have the internet, and great clips of these once favorite shows on YouTube. Both of my parents were factory workers, working in Massachusetts factories working opposite shifts to help care for me until the dreaded day that my father moved out. I was devastated. My father is 11 yrs. My mother's elder was very childlike in many ways. My mother was a very loving and kindhearted soul, but she did not pick men that were that way with her. As much as I loved my father even as a child, I knew he was more immature than the old soul in me. He worked hard yet played even harder. The love of gambling, having a few nips as he would call it, playing golf and running around was all my mother could take, even though he was the love of her life.

I felt her pain. Empaths are deep feelers. I was 4 years old when this happened. In these times of great awakenings, those who are connected in the now are aware of the light workers activations going on in the world today. Notice the increased action, people are speaking up, speaking their truths, asking questions. They can no longer hide, subdue, ignore, pretend, or brush off that gut kick that something is amiss or off. People are wanting to tune inward to connect with their higher selves. Make their lives better, shift their vibrational levels to match what feels right to them. Being a highly empathic person was a curse to my life in many ways in the past. I was always surrounded by left brained analytical people who did not understand me at all. I am right and left brained, some may call it psychic, somnambulism, strange, kooky, tin-foil hat, or eccentric. What I thought was a curse is a huge gift. The reason those people were in my life was to teach me to go deeper and I planted the seed of curiosity within them. Some were lost causes, and some were not.

I see how disconnected our society has become and how disconnected people have become from their own emotions. This saddens me on a deep level, and why I feel the world's pain. I had to learn how to live in this world and survive being so sensitive. I am not here to drown in others misery, I am here to light a fire to show others the way out. I can help those who feel lost because of sensitivities, those who want to feel more empathy for others, and those who want to grow spiritually within themselves. I can help you understand things that others do not. I already know that those searching for answers are already consciously connecting to the words I speak. How do I know? Well, I have been talking about this book for 10 years and I heard in my head "do it now! Now is the time!"

You may have heard stories of people having a flight scheduled to go somewhere and for some reason they were stopped from going, or felt that overwhelming urge that they just could not get on that plane? Then later find out that the plane crashed. When I was living in California, I was attending the Hypnosis College in Tarzana. One afternoon as I was driving up the grade headed towards Thousand Oaks, this is a several lane highway, the 101, that gets a lot of traffic, and there was a truck ahead of me that had these long metal pipes that it was hauling. I did not like the look of it or the way that the truck was carrying them (I could feel it was not good). I kept my eyes on this. The traffic was bumper to bumper on both sides of me as I was pinned in the middle lane. As I watched, to my horror, as the truck got close to the top of the hill several of those pipes came flying towards me. My first thought was "oh my God I am dead." I then got an overwhelming feeling that assured me that I was not going to die. It told me to stay the course, do not veer, do not swerve into other lanes. I call this the angel wash. Those pipes hit just in front of my moving vehicle and in amazement I watched them hit the ground and veer off to the right over the car on my right and down an embankment. Had I acted out of fear and veered in either direction or stopped I would have caused a major highway pile up. My inner knowing, my intuition, has saved me many times in my life, and this is just one of the times it has kept me safe.

You can learn to listen to this inner knowing too. Through my journey I have learned the ins and outs, how's and why's, and how to find my own solutions from my own inner knowing. I learned the hard way because growing up I was told not to talk about such things. This of course made me even more curious. Some people are content with complacency and just want to continue what they are doing and want nothing more. My father was one of those people and that is perfectly fine. I was born with the fire in me and have a vastly different path! I was born sensitive. However, we all can tune in, no matter what level you may think you are at.

Here is something to consider: Are you capable of learning how to play a musical instrument? Of course you could. The answer is a resounding yes, you can. With practice most anyone can. Some are just naturally good at something that others are not. What I am telling you is that you are born feeling, seeing, and hearing. You can learn to listen to your own inner voice with practice, patience, and persistence to the best of your own unique ability. So, what began as "shhh, do not talk about that" turned into "let us explore that!"

I have always been that person that others just tell everything going on in their lives to, the person who listens and does their best to help. I can be standing in line at a grocery store and come away with knowing a complete stranger's life's story. I can show you how to navigate those things that you may not realize are affecting you at a very deep core. I turned what I used to call my hobby into my business. Why did I call it a hobby? I listened to those who did not understand me and felt their doubt, not my own. Now, did I have my own set of doubts yes, I did. I worried because I was sensitive. I noticed the worry in my financial sense of security, and why was that? I grew up poor, I watched my single parent struggle to support my sister and I. It was not until the work that I was doing became mundane, unfulfilling, stagnant, missing important parts of life for me at my core that I got the courage to make the change. I did and I have never looked back.

I found me, myself, and my purpose in life. I have been working as a professional intuitive for over 14 yrs. getting paid for my advice and readings. You may have seen me on TV, in massive internet ads and just did not know it. I have a confidential contract with a major network; However, I have been practicing my whole life. I have used my intuition in all areas of my life. I am also a professional hypnotist, certified in therapy for making positive changes in people's lives, a comedy stage hypnotist that does shows. Laughter and connection are important to feeding my soul energy so I may give back to others. Through these chapters you will learn to navigate, connect, and tune into your own knowing. As I stated before, we are all individuals, and your experience will be your own unique one. It could be remarkably like what I describe here or something different.

Last statement of this chapter is: Are you one of those people who have been hiding because of how others perceive you? When you are sensitive and connected you feel their feelings, but I ask you, are they yours? Here you will learn through the chapters how to navigate that without the decades it took me to learn through life's school of hard knocks.

# Chapter 2

## Deja Vu: My life as an empath

When I was four years old my father abandoned us. After he left, I began to astral travel at night in my sleep. At that time, I did not know that was what I was doing, remember, I was only four. The sleepwalking stopped about that time, but the astral travel was just beginning. I missed my father very much and, in my sleep, my subconscious mind would search for his energy to connect to. Sometimes I would feel like I was walking around in my grandma Sara's apartment. That is where my father went to live after he and my mother split. Grandmother Sara was a French maid in real life. I will often kid about my grandmother being a French maid, but it is not the visual most conjured up in their minds. Instead, picture a very staunch religious woman armed with a rosary! She immigrated from Canada to the US in the 30's. She worked for a very wealthy Jewish lawyer her entire working career as a US citizen and was in her late 90's when she passed.

Although my grandmother could hardly speak any

English, I could figure out what she was trying to tell me. She was very Catholic, always prayed, went to church, and always carried a rosary with her. Communication between us was challenging, and it was difficult for her to understand me. Thankfully, my father would translate what I was saying to her. Because of her strict religious beliefs, I knew my father was not saying the exact things I was saying.

Growing up, I would watch Grandma Sara prepare a money package every month and send it to the church in Canada. She would then prepare a money package for the church here in the states. I would ask with great curiosity what she was doing with the money, and why she had to send some to both places. My father explained to me that she was helping the church do the lord's work. But somehow, she felt she always had to send money for prayer. This felt foreign to me for some reason. I understood and was ok with tithing to help others in need, I just did not believe that the priests would not pray for her or her family without sending money. She religiously sent 10% of her earnings to the church on a regular basis. There was always a special, or different vibe at Grandma Sara's house, one that I never felt with my other Grandma. I remember sitting with Grandma Sara and she was showing me things that she wanted me to have when she died. I was the first grandchild. I remember her showing me a long box that held her hair that was braided. It was at least 2 feet long before she cut it off. I remember looking at her thick beautiful raven braid and instantly began visualizing Native Americans/Canadian Indians as I gazed at it. Call it Deja Vu, or whatever it was, it was very vivid in my mind's eye and left an everlasting impression within me.

One of my fondest childhood memories was watching Grandma Sara dance. She loved to dance the Polka. This is who, and where, I got my inspiration and love for dance. Although she never understood the "Indian" thing, I would always feel the native connection with her.I did find out after ancestry DNA that I do have Native Ancestry and it comes from Sara's side of the family. This gives validation to the Deja vu experiences that I was having.

My native roots come from the Mi'kmaq (Mig Maw) tribe. They are a First Nations people of the Northeastern Woodlands indigenous to the areas now known as Canada's Atlantic Provinces. This region is also known as the Gaspé Peninsula of Quebec, as well as the northeastern region of Maine. My French ancestry comes from the Arcadians. I was a bit skeptical about using a DNA lab and I am not in any way advocating ancestry or DNA testing, as they are not using it solely for the purposes that they state. I am not happy that I took it and I struggled whether I should or not, but I knew it was the only way I was going to confirm my native blood, so I did begrudgingly. I knew though, without logically knowing, without any validation, through my father and grandmother, about the native ancestry.

This was my father's side of the family. I remember they were very hush hush and quite about personal things. I always knew Grandma Sara suffered deeply after the death of her husband, but I also knew there was a lot of underlying pain there too that none of them talked about. I was led to believe that my grandfather died of a heart attack, I found out later in life that was not true. I found out through my Aunt Janet in 2012 that it was something quite different. It is even deeper than what Aunt Janet knew as well. I am still working on that whole story as my own psychic detective.

After my parents divorced, I began spending much more time with my maternal grandmother, Alice. My Grandma Alice was the daughter of a Seven-Day-Adventist preacher. I adored both of my grandmothers. I must say that with Sara being a devout Catholic and Alice an earnest SDA, there were times when I was subject to very opposite spectrums and confusion with each of their beliefs. I eventually learned how to walk in both worlds so to speak. Both of my grandmothers were upset when my parents split because they knew how much my mother and father loved each other, it was just too hard for them to be together.

I love the time I spent with Grandma Alice. We would sit together for hours while she would teach me how to crochet. She was an expert at fancywork. She had this uncanny ability to produce beautiful creations without any type of pattern. She could reproduce something just by looking at the item. She taught me how to do the same. She could also grow a garden like no one's business and could bake like a master chef. I attribute my creative abilities to her. She knew I loved animals and she let me keep Jojo, my black kitten, at her house. I used to put Jojo in my baby doll carriage and in the basket of my bike as we would embark on our neighborhood adventures. I am remarkably attuned to cat energy, and people sometimes call me the cat whisperer. They are my spirit animal. I learned the depth of pure evil in the world the day some cold-hearted human hit my cat purposely. I still relish the fond memories of my little Jojo, she will always be in my heart.

From time to time Grandma Alice would send me up to the clearing in the meadow along the stream to pick wild blueberries for pies, muffins, and jams. I loved to go out into the meadow. It seemed that whenever I went there the animal kingdom would show up as well. I never knew who or what would show up, but I was always, or shall I say "mostly" excited to see them. I loved the deer, did not mind the raccoons, loved the birds, the foxes did not bother me either. I was a little leery of the skunks, for good reason. I was also taught that whenever I heard crashing of tree's to "RUN LIKE HELL" because it was a moose barreling through the woods like a locomotive at full steam, and you did not want to get in their sight.

As I would so often come running through the back

door for safety, Grandma Alice would laugh and ask, "what chased you out today?" I would tell her what animal it was, and she would say "you just draw them to you." It was just like Dr. Dolittle. At that age I did not understand it was an energy thing, I just knew I loved nature, except the mosquito's, black flies, and ticks. Every now and then my grandfather and uncle would return from the woods with a dead deer. I would always be devastated that they killed Bambi. I would stay mad at them for a while, as in my mind as a small child, it was horrible to me.

These memories are from between the ages of four to six, before the critical mind filter had begun to show, form and grow. I was still an open canvas. What is the critical mind filter you ask; I find this to be a good definition from the internet. I will say that, in my observation, for most people it develops between 8-9 yrs.

About Critical Filter

- It is that part of our mind which filters out the information being stored in our subconscious mind, as well as filtering out the information we retrieve from our subconscious mind
- Infants and newborns do not have very well-developed critical filter
- It develops between ages 2-8. That is why they are easily susceptible to impressions and influences
- Infants and children are also quick learners because of the inadequately developed critical filter.

I was still at the age of learning at lightning speeds, fearless about life on many levels, just wanting to grow and learn as much as possible. Most everything was a test, and a learning. You know those things you have a fear of and do not know why?

I also found out, not too long ago, that back in the 1600s, during the Salem Witch Trials, at least one female from my lineage was accused of being a witch and was hung. If you recall, I also have a strong Irish lineage and at that time the Irish brought over and used various herbal and natural remedies through different things in nature and the forest. Some of their rituals and traditions were different as well, and did not fit soundly with the conventional beliefs of the times. Unfortunately, many Irish immigrants were accused of witchcraft and hung, or burned at the stake because of this. In 2011 I took my mother to the Witch Museum located in Salem. She was absolutely amazed and loved looking at all the artifacts and stories. I didn't think I would ever get her out of there. My mother was beautiful and adorned with classic Irish green eyes and red hair. When I told my cousin Lisa how my mother reacted at the museum, she chuckled and said, "ask Uncle Bobby about the woman in our family who was hung as a witch." My Uncle has been working on the family tree, on the Irish side of our family, for a while now. Uncle Bobby is doing a great job, and I recently found out I even have relatives that fought in the civil war for the Union Army.

In 1994 I moved to Rome, Italy. The moment I stepped foot on the ground in Rome I knew I had been there before. I lived in Italy from 1994 until 1997 and then again from 1999 to 2001, for a total of six years of my life. Pompeii was emotional for me to visit, so was the Coliseum. The Vatican was a whole different story! I felt the prayers of generations there along with the Sistine Chapel. The size of the statues in the Vatican made you feel like an ant on the earth, or at least that is the way it was feeling to me.

Now what was the purpose of these stories? The point of all of this is to show you what it is like to be an Empath. There are many distinct levels, and these stories show you my connection. My connection with the Earth through animals, plants, and geographic locations. There are some places that I just could never live. It would physically affect my well being immensely. Have you ever, all of a sudden, out of nowhere, gotten a headache, and then a major storm took place, or an earthquake? I have, all throughout my life. These are just a few of the way's empaths are affected and, more often than not, do not understand why. Pay attention and you will see patterns begin to form.

When I lived in Japan, I never felt the connection of Deja Vu there. However, what I did feel was the constant earth shifts. I would drive my children crazy with waking them up at night to get into a safe place because I knew there was going to be a major earthquake! The problem was, I just did not know when it was going to happen. My employees would look at me like I was crazy sometimes when I would say "did you feel that?" They would say no. It was the shifts under my feet that I was constantly feeling. I have always felt that in LA and Burbank California. The quake happened in Japan only years later in 2011. The Volcano in Naples Italy will go too. Scientists are constantly watching that one. I could never live in LA; the energy is just too intense for me. I can visit for short periods of time and that is it. Just like Japan, I loved the people, but it was the earth that I always felt off with there.

Have you ever visited someplace and felt yucky, and did not know why? Pay attention to this. It is not your vibration. I believe it is your own instinct telling you it is not at your level. If you try to force it you will always feel stuck, or in limbo. I am a deep sensor, and it is important for me to step into the energy and feel what it feels like to my psyche. Don't learn the hard way and let others convince you of being in a place that does not feel right to you. Those fleeting feelings you get of good or bad, pay attention to them! For this is your own psychic center. In the world of disconnecting on an emotional and psychical level it is destroying our own natural ability to sense what is good for us and what is not. The more we seem to get into technology the less healthy we become and the more disconnected we become. It is so important for an Empath to disconnect from electronics and connect with the earth to ground. I walk in nature every day. If I do not do this, I will become sick with the overload of information and garbage that is being thrown at us daily through the media. If you have children, please become aware of the effects these things have on them. Even animals respond. Nurture in nature, breath in the fresh air, connect to each other one on one. Limit the cell phone and internet time for them and you. Trust me, you will become much happier. Calming or upbeat music that is kind is best as it keeps the smiles coming. Even animals respond well to what you are listening to. If you want to know if it is good for you, watch how animals respond to it.

When someone tells you, even a child, about feeling like they have been in a certain place or situation, ask for details. They could be describing a past life to you... If you believe in that sort of thing. You should do the same for yourself. Children are open to energies, like little sponges they absorb everything around them. Everything they see, feel, and hear. Their minds are open to form. Their little critical mind filter has yet to form. They believe in Santa Claus, magic, love cartoons, bright colors, and music.

I have known too many people that have had these experiences. These feelings or intuitions can also be about places and events about to happen. Again, it all comes from our own perspective and what we ourselves see. Could it be a solution that is being presented to you about a situation and your mind is bringing it to you through intuition? We are all connected, and we are born feeling.

Our body is just the case that surrounds our soul. Embrace those feelings like the mind of a child in wonder and openness.

# Chapter 3

## Lightning Calling

I call these my antenna alignment activation years. Can you imagine answering the phone as a five-year-old thinking someone was calling, only to be zapped with an electrical shock? Remember, I was only five years old! I was visiting my grandparents on the farm in Maine. They had one of those old black rotary phones which had a party line. I used to love listening to others talk and I would get into trouble with Grandma Alice for listening in on others through the party line. Well, the phone rang during a summer thunderstorm one evening, and I got all excited and jumped up to answer it. Much to my surprise it was not a person calling, it was the lightning. Those old phone lines were not grounded back then. It must have only been seconds, but it felt like hours of me not being able to let go of the phone. Grandma was working in the shoe factory so I was there with Grandpa and it scared the ever-living heck out of him. After I was able to let go of the phone, he saw the sheer terror in my eyes and my little body shaking. He picked me up and rocked me in the rocking chair as I cried and shook. He did not know what to do with me and I knew it. He just rocked me, petted my back until I calmed down and fell asleep from the life-threatening thing I just went through. He also did not want to get on grandma's bad side for allowing anything to happen to me, or worse yet, my mother's. He did make a call to old doctor Gould, who my mother called the old horse doctor, and he took me down to see him. We did not tell Grandma because she would be mad at both of us. You will never catch me answering a phone in a lightning storm now!

I was just a fearless kid not realizing the dangers of that whole scenario, but I was not supposed to be answering the phone and I just did it thinking it was a safe thing for me to do. The morale of the story is that what appears innocent and safe on the outside can be deadly. Like when you are told do not touch the hot stove and then you do it and get burnt! That one was a favorite of my son. We often think that warnings can be silly, and we do not pay attention to what others say, just brushing it off. Another empathic trait is that we tend to find routine, rules, or control, imprisoning; anything that takes away freedom is debilitating to an empath, even toxic. The ability to be a free spirit is paramount to feelers of the world. I could not tell my mother or grandmother what happened with the lightning as they would have really let Grampa and I have it. From that point on I was under the table every time we had a thunderstorm. To this day I still do not like them, it is something you do not want to mess with!

Having had varying paranormal experiences throughout my young life, as well as the NDE's (Near death experiences) and OBE's (Out of body experiences,) catapulted this incredibly young, unaware empath into the awakening period. Like I previously stated, my mother did not have good luck with picking men that were in her best interest. Her new man was very abusive to her and I was always on high alert. He would come for a few days, they would have a fight and he would leave for several days then come back when he thought the coast was clear. This is when my antenna grew. My little brain was always listening for the sound of my mother, even when I was sleeping. I believe this is the same connection mothers have with their babies, only this was just reversed.

You may know someone or something similar, or it may have even happened to you as a young child. You began to work things out in your child's mind for survival. You step into being your mother's protector to the best of your ability. You may always have felt this overwhelming urge to stay aware and alert. This person brought fear and uncertainty into your lives. Between the late nights, the alcohol, and the physical abuse that never seemed to end. I remember my mother getting us ready to move to Texas where she had a few brothers living at the time. Things took a quick turn once she found out she was pregnant. She thought things would change and so she decided to stay. Well, to no one's surprise, it did not work out. It only got worse. I started to get teased at school because I was getting stye s in my eyes from lack of sleep. The teacher commented for me to use tea bags on my eyes for relief. This in turn led to my nickname, "Tea Bags." Kids can be so cruel.

My little sister was born when I was seven years old. My mother was so happy because she had red hair just like mom. Here is a little bit of coincidence: She was born one day before my birthday. Mom's birthday was in the same month a week later. We would all celebrate together. I was born the 7th, my sister on the 6th, and our mother on the 14th. I was born 7, my sister and I are 7 years Apart, and our mother's birthday is 7 days from mine. Pay attention to the little things that you may say "oh that is just a coincidence." My sister and I were both born in Clinton, Massachusetts, my grandmother was born in Clinton, NY and my mother lived in Clinton, Maine for many years and is now buried there. How about this; my stepbrother Scott now lives in Clinton, Massachusetts! How many coincidences or things like this do you have in your life? We are all connected, and the world really is a small place if you are paying attention to all those connections.

I always kept my eyes and ears peeled for my mother and baby sister. Thankfully, the mayhem did calm down for a brief period but then it started up again. My mother worked long hours to support us while he only worked the summer months and was off in the winter. Winter was always the worst season as he drank and stayed out late only to come home and start beating on my mother. I was not big enough to fight him, but I was smart enough to get out of the house and run to a neighbor for help. Once that happened, he would flee and stay gone for days at a time. I learned to be sly like a fox to protect my mother. I once watched my mother get super strength that I never knew she had. He had chased her into the bedroom, she then reached under the bed in a flash and pulled out a bed slat in the blink of an eye and went after him with it! That time she was able to get him out of the house. My eyes must have been huge. Have you ever experienced or witnessed the superpowers we all have within us once that adrenaline rush kicks in? It is impressive and something I have never forgotten. We ended up moving yet once again. This last fight before we were on the run, he had my mother by the throat backed up against the wall. She was bright red and I could feel the life draining out of her. I don't even know where this came from, but I kicked him from behind as hard as I could in the testicles and then I ran like the wind down flights of stairs and to the next-door neighbors to call for help! He did take off. His pattern was to take my mother's catalytic converter off of her car so she could not leave when he would take off like this. Luckily, my grandfather and uncle worked on cars, so they brought one over for her car and we packed the whole house up and moved to the state of Maine. He must have been shocked when he returned to an empty house. My mother knew he would end up killing us if we stayed. My little sister was only 4 when we left. My mother was only married to him for 6 months. For some reason she felt that if they got married, he would change. How many times have you seen that story play out, or you may have done something similar? Luckily for us my mother realized that we were in grave danger and she got us all out of this treacherous situation. She listened to her gut, her intuition, instead of trying to rationalize various things in her head of why he was doing this to us and then professing love. My sister did not know or remember these events, and my mother was happy for that. My little sister was always so sensitive and sweet, and Mom never ever spoke bad of her father. I did not either. It would be too hurtful; as children we pick up on stuff, thinking maybe somehow we are at fault. Of course, that was never the case. So, my sister and I basically lost our fathers at the same time. Although mine would come every so often for a visit, it was far and few between. He was in Massachusetts and I was in Maine. We could not move back because of the violence.

Have you ever had a life threatening experience that awakened a different level of awareness in you, like you have never felt before? It ignites that deep level of just knowing that you cannot explain it to others. It is hard for others to comprehend unless they have experienced something similar. So, when your life receives a lightning bolt jolt for awareness, however it comes, it truly changes the way you view the world around you.

Once, while flying out of Orlando, Florida, our flight was grounded for hours until a severe storm cleared the area. Once we finally boarded our plane and got airborne, that storm was still close by. I will never forget the sick feeling I got just thinking about the storm still being close by, and the way lightning streaked through the sky! What if lightning strikes the plane? I desperately prayed, "Please God get us out of here please safely." It felt like we were going to fall out of the sky. I was literally sick after the drop of the plane and all the turbulence. I take cover the best I can when lightning comes knocking. On the positive side of things though, I have a feeling that lightning jolt awakened an even deeper sensitivity in me somehow, and I have even joked about how that is what is wrong with me.

# Chapter 4

# Old Souls, New souls, and Connections

Have you ever been told you are an old soul? There are many definitions of old souls by various people over the decades. We are all born with one. Our physical body is the case for the soul we are born with. I was one of those kids that hung out with adults. I always felt more comfortable with adults than I did with other children. Just maybe you have felt this way too. I was always told I was wise beyond my years, yet at that time I just smiled and took note of things going on around me. Now don't me wrong, I had friends, but adults resonated with me more. If you investigate definitions of reincarnation, it is when a soul returns in a new life form in a new lifetime with a different goal. There are those who foster the belief that our souls continue to reincarnate until we have learned the lessons set forth from the lifetimes before.

New souls are considered to be just born or with only a few past lives. I came in with many lifetimes under my belt. One of my favorite books is titled *Astrology for the*

*Soul*, by Jan Spiller. In it, she seems to be describing my journey in life to a tee. She writes: "Most babies are born naked, but not these folks! Born wearing ten shirts, fourteen sweatshirts, twelve pairs of pants and a half dozen overcoats. They bring all their past life burdens with them."

Here are some signs you may be an old soul.

- You enjoy being alone and need some alone time to thrive, you have a good grasp of reality and realize life is short.
- Common sense is your forte.
- Knowledge is something you thirst for. Always learning and seeking the truth even if it hurts.

I have always been more spiritual than what others may call religious. I believe in God, have seen angels, and have heard the angelic choir. I never feel alone, even when I am obviously physically alone. I have always been a deep thinker, not a crowd follower. Not to say I do not have a tribe, I most certainly do. In this time of universal transition, more and more souls like me are coming forward and speaking out. I never really felt like I fit in as a child, therefore I found myself connecting to the spirit world more than this physical reality we are all experiencing. My mother knew of my "special gifts," but would brush them off and pretend they were just part of my silly childhood imagination.

Have you noticed that people just come up and start telling you their stories without even knowing you? How about that feeling you just know them. Well, I believe you do! Your soul knows their soul from past lives. My uncle Peter, who is seven years older than me, had a friend named April who used to take me around with her. Again, I always seemed to be more comfortable with the older people. April worked at a nursing home in the small rural town I was living in. The residents of the nursing home just loved me. April would make statements about how they would light up when they saw me, and they would even tell me things about themselves that she never knew about them. Over time these visits started to get very heavy for me. I did not realize that they knew I could see, hear, and feel. I noticed over time a pattern had developed with many of the elderly. Some of them would seem light or almost too transparent for me to me to even see at times. These people would be the ones passing on in the near future. Of course, I had no idea at that time what that meant, and it just seemed to feel natural to me until I started putting two and two together. I would get so upset every time one of them passed as I could feel the loss from their loved ones and the fear in others. As a 13-year-old empath who had no rational idea why this was happening, eventually it overwhelmed me. Because of this, I had to stop going to the nursing home with April.

Sometimes I would cry for days, unaware that I was feeling the pain of others. Because I had no idea how to control this, it pretty much controlled and consumed me to the point where I could not even attend a funeral. Today that is a different story, but back then there was no way. Have you ever felt so overwhelmed with grief and sadness, and realized it was not attached to you personally? I know when I talk about the fading and releasing of souls as they depart one's physical body, many doctors and nurses have also experienced this phenomenon and understand it. They may not express it the same way I do, but they see it as a stage that they rationalize in their minds regarding end of life situations. Some highly empathic doctors and nurses will even admit they have seen a soul leave the body. Many doctors and nurses are gifted, they just don't know it. It becomes automatic for them. During this time, I was confused, and I did not have someone like myself to talk to. I now help those that are crossing over, and I can now attend funerals. I have learned how to master certain things about who I am, yet I am still learning every day. We truly are connected if we just allow ourselves to step out of the overthinking chatterbox mind. Maybe this will ring true for you too. It could also be that you have noticed that you pick up on those getting ready to pass. Have you ever found yourself becoming overwhelmed in large crowds? Or a place you go to gives you a bad headache, and when you leave so does the headache. For me, this became an everyday way of life. While most teenagers were going to concerts, I chose to skip them. I went to a few but each time I got sick and emotionally overwhelmed, in turn it started giving me physical symptoms. My mother claimed I had anxiety. In a way I did, but it was not coming from me so much as from my surroundings and the people I was surrounded by. It is so important I have a peaceful home. I do not fare well around chaotic people and I just have to walk away and say no. You see, this is something empaths have a problem doing. They are naturally healers and givers. It just goes against the word no.

As I mentioned earlier, you do not need a lifetime of learning every long hard step. That is, of course, unless you want to. We tend to want peace and will do our best to help create that. I do have to say, once an empath has had enough, it's usually a done deal for the other person completely. This is because empaths tend to hang on so long that by the time they give up, it's out of complete exhaustion. Also, the emotions concerning the situation or person change so drastically that there really is no return. It's usually a healing, a lesson and a growth period that just takes place. Please do yourself and your soul a huge favor and learn to forgive. Like I said, you do not forget, but for you to move forward you have to be forgiving. If you do not, it will just get stuffed and continue to fester just under the surface.

I was not very forgiving about having to move to another state or having to live out in the country. We did not have the comforts we had before the move, and I saw this small Maine town as behind the times compared to where I had come from. This also affected me in school. I was the strange new kid from out of state. I managed to make it through Jr. High, and I made quite a few friends. Being sensitive does not necessarily mean you are introverted. I was a child of the 70's. I remember watching a family friends' daughter who was so high on acid that we stayed locked downstairs in their house for a whole day. She hallucinated and cried. It was one of the scariest things I had seen and felt. She literally thought things were attacking her. I did not want her to get into trouble and she begged for me to stay with her, so I did. I was horrified, yet it was one of the best things to witness at my young age. It kept me from ever doing that. I tried pot a few times. Back then it seemed like everyone was doing it. I soon learned that it was not my cup of tea. The pot just made me paranoid, lazy and hungry. I did not like the way it made me feel so I lost interest. The vice I chose was good ole alcohol. It did not take much for me to feel its effects as I was light weight. Have you noticed though that sensitives, empaths will choose something to soothe? You really have to be careful or you may find yourself in trouble without even realizing how you ever got there to begin with.

We are the feelers, the canaries of the world. The world seems to want to place us in a mold. Many of us also have to watch our carbs as we can put on body armor fast. We are also particularly prone to autoimmune issues. It's challenging at times because we are independent and rebellious by nature. Have you ever had a teacher or boss get angry with you because you did not perform a lesson or task their way? You performed the lesson or task completely, but you performed it your way? Here's a true story with my high school English teacher. English was one of my favorite subjects at one time, but that changed. Her name was Ms. Griffin. You see, I would do this thing that I was not aware of, and it would send her off the rails. I would go into a state of trance in class. This was my way of learning and connecting. She would get angry and yell at me and as always it broke the state of trance. When that happened, she would tell me in a huff and a puff to go to the principal's office. I had no clue why other than I would roll my eyes when I came out of trance and she would get upset. I would gather my books to go to the principal's office, he'd ask why I was there, and I would explain I was not sure but one thing I did know was that I irritated her to no end therefore she did not like me. I was never disrespectful, she just could not wrap her head around that it was the way I learned. The principle was nice, he just told me to study there until the bell and then go to my next class.

That was a year that set the tone for the remainder of my school years. I really enjoyed learning and always loved to do schoolwork. However, after this treatment I just rebelled and stopped paying attention. I always passed but I could have done so much better. I excelled in Jr. High and my English teacher, Ms. Smith, loved me. When you are a feeler it really affects you. I did not understand why, and I certainly did not know how to change it other than just retreat and stay out of sight as much as possible. I was always pretty mellow unless attacked, and then it was a different story. The old survival mode would kick in and even though I have a small stature I can be a big handful for some people. I look back at this whole situation and, instead of letting her get to me that way, I should have proved her wrong. I learned later how to confidently do just that. She just did not understand me, and I did not understand why she was so irritated with me at the time. I now know it was a past life thing with her and me. She had these very deep dark eyes and hair, and I could feel her on a soul level. I would hear people talk about nuns. I feel she may have been one in a past life, and a gypsy in another! When you are a free spirit you will notice that you irritate some people for just breathing. These are those people that feel they have to control everyone and everything. Your energy, spirit and soul say a different thing and they want to put out your passion. Don't ever let them. There is a saying "misery loves company" and it's true. Rise above it because we do attract like vibrations to us. The dark is attracted to the light, but so is the light. Stay in the light, visualize you are protected and affirm that you are every day. Ask your guides, angels and God to protect, guide and help you to be the person you came here to be. One thing that I have learned is the power of prayer is so powerful and it is something that we can do every day for ourselves and others.

# Chapter 5

# Empathic Impressions

In the previous chapter we talked about old souls. We old souls seem to be adults as kids and get more youthful as we age. Have you noticed yourself feeling that way? One of the hardest things for an empath to do is allow someone to hurt themselves. Why? Because we are natural healers, and we tend to want to fix people. Usually, we end up damaging ourselves because we deplete our own energy in order to help others. This is one of the reasons I have been wanting to write this for over a decade. If I can help a young empath understand why they feel the way they feel, experience the unexplainable, and see or hear things that are not of the physical, this book will save them years of stress and setbacks. There are so many things that will affect you. There are many levels of empathic gifts. Some have this intense feeling of earth energies. These people are known as geopathic empaths. I happen to be one. I will get bariatric headaches when there are storms coming. I will also feel the earth under my feet with upcoming earthquakes. One of the scariest things to me is the feel of an impending tornado. Even the animal kingdom runs for cover! Have you ever noticed these things tied to weather with yourself? If you have, then you connect to the earth's energies. I personally have never met an empath that is not connected to the animal kingdom.

Have you ever walked into a place and it just felt wrong to you? The energy was heavy, thick, and sickly feeling. I remember going to Detroit in the early 90's. I got off the plane and I remember saying to my girlfriend that I was visiting how heavy it felt there and it made me so depressed the whole time I was there. What I was picking up on was the death of Detroit and how the city crumbled in the 90's. When I arrived back in Maine the energy just shifted. Looking back at my childhood, I remember my grandmother being upset with me because I did not want to wear second hand clothes from the thrift store. She thought I was just so spoiled. It was way more than that. No matter what I said about how it made me feel she just was not accepting that answer. She raised seven children in the depression and knew too well just what poverty was. I even told my mother I did not like the way the clothes felt to me. Now, I could wear something that belonged to a friend or family member I knew and trusted, but there was way too much negative energy in thrift store garments. My mother was a single mom, I started working at 12 in the summers so I could help buy my own school clothes. That is how much it meant to me not to wear other people's energy. No matter how much I tried to explain it, they just did not get what I was talking about. This is like how certain people can hold and object and connect to things about where it came from and who it belonged to. This is called Psychometry.

According to Wikipedia Psychometry, also known as token-object reading, or psychoscopy, is a form of extrasensory perception characterized by the claimed ability to make relevant associations from an object of unknown history by making physical contact with that object. Supporters assert that an object may have an energy field that transfers knowledge regarding that object's history. There is no scientific evidence that psychometry exists, and the concept has been widely criticized. I have been in groups where we will hold an item with closed eyes from an unknown person and see what we can feel. I have witnessed some amazing connections. Some people did not connect, but the empaths that are gifted with reading energy imprints certainly were quite remarkable. I always cleanse and clear new items and stones that I bring into my home. If I have an item from others, I just clear them with sage and positive intentions. There are so many things that happen in this world that are unexplainable to our logical minds. I used to get frustrated because, when I was young, I just thought everyone knew what I knew, or could feel what I was feeling. There are some really gifted empaths that can remove heavy pain and energy from others. I can feel other emotions and, at times, their physical pain as well. Have you just ever found yourself feeling like something is wrong with someone that you know? You have this overwhelming urge to check on them only to find out that there was indeed a crisis going on? Then there are those things you just seem to know without knowing how. Some people would say to me "oh you are just shooting from the hip;" my response was always "no, I am going with my gut. Why do you ask?" I learned to stop questioning what sets you and your spiritual growth back. Just go with it. I have made many mistakes over thinking, but never when I went with my gut. Your gut feeling is your super sensor antenna and it will never lead you astray.

I have always been a walker since I can remember. Walking is just as important as breathing to me. It took many years for me to understand why I need to do this. I am not a typical 'Om' meditator. I meditate by walking and connecting to nature. I ground and center with my walks. I just let myself connect to nature. You may even find me talking to animals on my walks. I'm sure at times some people would think "is that woman talking to herself?" I have discovered that I have a native guide. When I am supposed to know something, he sends in the animals until I pick up the message that I am supposed to get. This is how my connection works, yours may work differently. Your guide will make a connection to you however they can, but you have to figure out your system of connecting.

Yes, you do have a guide, and a guardian angel too. Some of us have more than one guide. For many years, whenever I connected to a person like myself with medium skills, they would ask if I knew there was a big Indian around me. I would say I knew I was somehow connected to native traditions, until the day I saw his shadow following me on my walk. I almost passed out. I was on my daily walk when I was living in southern California. This walk took me through this little park close to where I used to live. I was just walking and then I got the feeling something was very close to me and I looked to my right and saw this huge shadow and, no, it was not mine, it was a big Native American man in full headdress. I froze and I thought "ok, do I dare turn around or do I just keep walking?" I had to turn around and then I saw nothing, just the thought in my mind saying, "I had to show you my presence now get to work and stop over thinking." I get feathers when I have been elevated in spiritual growth. You may notice things that you get.

We are all individuals and we have that soul we came in with. It is a physical journey of reaching God's purpose for us in this lifetime. We all come into the physical with a purpose, a reason to be here on this earth for however long we are slated to be here. Only the divine plan and the divine know when we will return home. Have you ever noticed that some people are just so afraid of death? I have this sense that when it is my turn to leave that I will be met and guided. Once you have a near death experience you just seem to realize it's just the spirit continuance. I have also felt the spiritual presence of family members coming for a person that is getting ready to leave the planet. They may have conversations with people who have already passed before them. They may even tell you that they were just speaking to someone you know is deceased. My father was a gambler, hence the reason he never had anything in life but debt and lived day by day. When he was getting ready to pass, he was talking to his bookie! Now his bookie had been deceased for a long time. When my father retired his social security barely covered the rent, let alone even thinking about betting. My sons found that confusing, but I knew what was happening. Have you ever witnessed this with a loved one or friend? If you have not, at some point in your life you will, and it's pretty amazing to watch. Of course, your logical mind is going no, no, no that cannot be. If you find yourself doing this, stop! It will slow your growth way down spiritually. I know this is hard to explain or talk to others about for many of us, but trust me, you will find your tribe of people that will understand.

I have learned to have faith because we are all presented with spiritual teachers. They show up at the right time every time. As you begin to pay attention to the way things just are for you, you will begin to hone one thing at a time. Some people are only sensitive to certain energy, others are gifted in more than one area. Do not worry about that, just focus on what it is that is there in front of you in the now. Life will send you what you are supposed to be learning at the time you are supposed to learn. All too often though, we want, or even try, to force a timing issue. I love the saying "Let go and let God." In other words; it will happen when it's supposed to happen. You cannot force the petals of a flower to open, they open on the universe's time.

Now, I will say we do have choices in life. Some people never want to hone or listen to the urges, nudges, or feelings. They will often medicate with alcohol, drugs (prescription or street) and even food. There are empaths that get big because they are trying to constantly ground themselves with food. Carbs are comfort foods, and this serves as body armor. I know that some of you may know someone who is very gifted, or it may even be you that is constantly battling keeping their weight in check. This is another reason. Some feel the pain and do not understand it's not them, so they take on that energy and drink the pain away. There is a reason they call alcohol spirits. It is your soul crying out for a spiritual connection. There is a reason AA is a spiritually based program. There must be a belief of a higher power no matter your religion. Drug and alcohol abuse only open portals for negative energies.

I feel that I was always protected from that bad life choice. Growing up, I watched so many friends and family members have negative reactions to these illicit drugs that just being around them while they went through their experiences made me say no thank you. I managed to survive as a child of the 70's and thankfully never got into the cocaine rage of the 80's either. My choice was alcohol.

Luckily, I was able to wake myself out of that trance before I became one of those statistics. Sadly, I lost family members and friends to it though. It is so painful to watch as an empath that, if we do not disengage completely, it can overwhelm us to a point of making us physically sick.

One thing I have learned the hard way is that being an empath can seem like a superpower to others yet to you feels like a curse at times. Although most people can get a sense of how others may be feeling, empaths seem to take it to a whole other level. We are all able to feel energy, yet the empath feels it on a much deeper level. At times, it's almost to the point of being overwhelming, and for some it can be life altering. When I was a teen, I would get so overwhelmed with anxiety that it would physically lock up my neck and shoulders. You know the old saying about carrying the weight of the world on your shoulders, well I literally did. My mother would drive me to the internist to get a shot. Whatever it was that he gave me relaxed me so I could move again. This was energy that I was picking up from others, I just had not evolved or understood that it was not mine to wear. I did figure out on my own that large crowds really set me off. I avoided those situations as much as possible. While my friends were going to live Rock concerts, I chose to stay home and enjoy listening to the music either on the radio or by playing my records. What I have learned through many trials is that when I start feeling overwhelmed energetically, I stop and ask in my mind "does this feeling belong to me or someone else?"

The moment I say those words now to myself, if it is not mine it leaves, if it's mine then I start to process what is going on in my life that can be causing these negative feelings.

During this time of my growth and development I had come to accept that I was sensitive, and that I liked being around older people. I also tried my best to hide what others would think of as strange or weird. I was doing the best I could to fit in with people in my age group. At that time, I had to push back and mentally shut off my medium abilities. I was just not mature enough and I just did not want to deal with these feelings for the time being. I also had no one that would listen to me without them telling me that it was just my imagination and these things weren't real.

So, for the time being, I would just tune out as much as I could. I found that I became exhausted and ran down quickly if I did not get enough sleep. As children we seem to have endless energy, and as teens we just burn both ends. I got so sick one year with mono that it put me in bed for months and out of school. I almost lost my spleen over it. I remember Mr. Halperin, our health class teacher, told the basketball team to stay away from me because I had the kissing disease. I was a cheerleader at the time and that just devastated me! Not only was I out of school and got behind, now I had a disease label. Between my health class teacher and my English teacher freaking out, I became completely turned off with school. Maybe you found yourself feeling this same way. It's like trying to fit a square peg into a round hole. Empaths are free spirits by nature so trying to control us causes things to happen depending on how we can navigate the turmoil caused by this. Protecting your space and having a calm environment is crucial to an empath to thrive and stay healthy.

## Chapter 6

## The Trance – Tuning In and Out

Realizing our own unique individual gifts can be a challenge. We have family and friends that tend to want to put either words of encouragement or words that take you away from creating the life you came here to complete. You must not take this personally. Some want to live vicariously through others without ever taking a risk to step out of the box themselves or they cannot see for you what they cannot see in themselves. Empaths have a challenging time with this. First of all, they tend to want to please and make others happy, and secondly, they want to fix other people's problems. Being a sensor makes a person want to fix what is not making them feel good, not only for themselves but for others. This is totally exhausting. Helping others is a wonderful gift to share. But the catch here is that they must want to fix it enough for themselves first. You are dealing with their pain and consequences. It exhausts you and does nothing for their growth. As I developed, I started to realize I attracted certain people to me. Takers can spot a giver a mile away. Being from a blue-collar working-class family with meager means can put you in a place of those who must take advantage of your current space in life. This includes all areas of your life. My mother was strict and protective of me. I was not let out of the house to date until I was 16 years old. I had a few close girlfriends and one thing I noticed emerging was from typical things girls will do. We would wear each other's clothes or try each other's make-up and jewelry. I had one friend that if she wore anything of mine clothes wise I could no longer wear that item when she gave it back. It got so bad that I found myself with hardly any clothes left. I explained earlier how I had felt about used clothes; I just was not able to explain why I felt that way. My friend realized that if she borrowed something from me that she really liked that she would end up with it. I would end up just giving it to her because I could not wear it. After losing most of my school clothes, and having no way of earning more money during the school year other than babysitting, I had to say no to loaning clothes out. Looking back, and looking at the path and circumstances that this friend had in life, I now know why. What a hard life full of pain she lived. This was the awareness that I was noticing, yet this certainly was not logical, nor could I explain to anyone why I felt that way. I was tuning in and the feeling was so intense, I chose to deal with it with compassion and love. I had to because it was so overwhelming to me that I could not ignore it without it making me an emotional mess to the point of getting sick. The dreaded word "no" to others can mean a big yes to you. Please do not ever feel guilty about saying yes to you. I know it is so hard to give to yourself when you are wired to give it all to others. One of the hardest lessons an empath must learn. Feeling guilty about being happy: what a crazy thought. As crazy as that sounds it is the walk of many. People find healing and light in you, so shine, without feeling guilty. This is a wonderful powerful quote I love *"Our deepest fear is not that we are inadequate. Our deepest fear is that we are powerful beyond measure. It is our own light, not our darkness, that most frightens us. We ask ourselves, who am I to be brilliant, gorgeous, talented, and fabulous? Who are you not to be? You are a child of God. Your playing small does not serve the world. There is nothing enlightened about shrinking so that other people will not feel insecure around you. We were born to manifest the glory of God that is within us. It is not just in some of us, it is in everyone. And as we let our light shine, we unconsciously give other people permission to do the same. As we are liberated from our own fear, our presence automatically liberates others."* - Marianne Williamson.

Fast forward to the first boyfriend I attracted. You know he was a major control freak, and his father was one with his mother. The alarms were going off all over the place. I had to move to my girlfriend's house next door when I broke up with this guy. He was so irrational that he even tried to run over my mother! So I put myself in a place where there was a big man telling him to get lost. Have you ever been in a situation that you know you will be put in harm's way unless you get the courage to move somewhere out of the way? It took several months for this guy to get his thoughts off me and on to someplace else. Thank God I listened to my intuition there.

My next relationship was a fast-moving train wreck. Instead of tuning in I was tuning out with attention that I was not used to getting. The guy was older, swept me off my feet and put me on a pedestal until after I married him. At that time, he moved me away from my friends and family. I am that woman that cheating men fear. I will always know. I only stayed with him for one year. I had to plan and sneak out. This man even became abusive and I am not the one that will stay, I will figure a way out. Never ever tell someone who is abusive or mentally ill what your plans are. Plan the escape and never look back. What I learned through my mother's heart ache saved me from staying with those who show you they will not change, it will only get worse. I made that escape and guess what, I went back to the same friend's parents' home temporarily until I could get a handle on what my next step would be.

My mother had remarried 2 weeks after I had, she had a new husband, my little sister and two step siblings in high school and I needed to figure it out. While I was there, I met the love of my life. This man just approached me out of nowhere at a local spot that I used to go. He had asked me about the Siamese kitten listing I had posted. He couldn't care less about the kittens, he only wanted to get the phone number off my listing. I got that gut kick and heard in my head that is your next husband. Now how ridiculous a thought that was I said to myself and I left and went home. Have you ever had an experience like that? I bet some of you reading this can relate. Later that evening the phone rang, and it was him, not calling for a kitten but calling for a date. That was in 1978. I divorced my first husband and married this man in 1981. Later that year I gave birth to our son. Now I just knew I was going to be married to this guy on a gut level. He certainly was not looking for marriage when we met but I knew, and I was just getting out of a crazy marriage. As things started to progress with our lives and a move from the east coast to the west coast in 1982, our lives changed in many ways.

We tend to be creatures of our upbringing in many ways. I had a very developed pulse on my child and my husband. The west coast was not good for our marriage and his father's influence certainly caused some riffs in our relationship. We were young and in love and figured love will get us through anything. My husband Denny loved his jeep and four wheeling. He was active duty military and into certain hobbies and things that a lot of men enjoy. There were several things that would cause arguments. The jeep was one of the major ones. I used to get bad feelings all the time with it. He was always sinking money into it after these four-wheeling events. He did major modifications to it that I certainly did not like. I started having dreams about accidents and that would really get me upset. The club that he started at the base we were stationed at thought I was just no fun at all. I would tell them someone is going to get hurt bad one of these times, and often I get laughed at. Have you ever had dreams that came true that were nightmares? Well, it began happening. You see, like I said, a man cannot hide cheating from me, I will know.

Here is where it began to fall apart. I noticed it and caught it, just like I have every other time in my life. Vehicle accidents started to happen, and he even had one with my son who was about 2 and half years old. When he brought Levi home with a concussion, I lost it. I went to seek counseling for a few months as I desperately needed someone to talk to. I even tried to get my husband to come with me, but he refused. I decided to leave the dreams of him dying in that jeep. It got too much for me to handle and I knew he still had contact with the other women. There was more than one and I knew it. I left him and headed to the east coast on New Year's Eve of 1985 with my son. I was tuning in because I knew on a gut level, I had to take a hard stance to shift this energy. This was the hardest and most painful thing I had ever done. I left the love of my life to hopefully get a positive outcome out of an unpleasant situation. I knew in my gut and heart he loved me the same way. He was brought up differently than I was. I was right again.

He caught up with me on Valentine's day begging for me to come back home. We met in Washington DC in March while he was there seeing his detailer to get back to the east coast. We made plans for me to come back until we would get another duty station. I wanted to see for sure how much he wanted it.

He came in April and picked up our son to take him back to California. I was to follow in a few weeks, giving my employer a two-week notice and getting the things we needed temporarily until the transfer. My son got to spend a few weeks alone with his father before his passing. Levi was 3.5 yrs. old when Denny died. Denny died in a four-wheel drive accident on April 21, 1985. I cannot begin to tell you the grief I felt. Have you ever beat yourself up so bad over something that you knew was going to happen, yet you did everything you could think of to prevent it, but it still happened? Denny knew himself. He used to tell me he would never see his 30$^{th}$ birthday, and I would get mad at him and tell him to stop that kind of talk. Well, it came true, he only lived to be 28 years old. My grief shut me down for years on an intuitive level. I did not want to listen or tune into anything after this. What I went through with his death, and his funeral, is something only horror stories are written about. Death can bring out the best or it brings the worst out in families and friends. For me it was the latter. I could not tell anyone about this except a few close friends. What I was experiencing was Claircognizance. Claircognizant empath's definition is a blend of emotional empathy and clear knowing. I also thought I had turned off medium connections at 13 after the nursing home experiences. I had just tuned them out. We all have choices in life, and it is our free will. At this time, I was so devastated with what had just happened I went into a deep level of grief. God knew he had to help us repair our torn relationship before he took Denny home. For that I will be forever grateful. I do not think I would have made it through myself had that not happened. Levi tried to wake his father at the service which totally set the whole church howling with tears. My little boy shut down and shut off like a switch. I had so much trouble sleeping between the headaches from crying all the time and then drinking wine at night to sleep. It's no wonder my head felt like it was about to explode. I felt like a part of me died that day, and it did on a soul level. I have never felt that kind of love connection again yet in this lifetime. On a soul level I know that what is supposed to happen will. Have you ever lost someone that you loved so much that it not only emotionally made you sick it took a toll on you physically? Soul connections are like no other; they are deep and hard to explain. Others with good intentions will say that it will get easier or better, just know that they mean well. In time, you adjust and accept the fact that they are gone. But for many people the missing and pain of losing that person you loved so much in life will never change. Guess what, it never changes with them either. The only thing we take with us is the love we created here on earth, or the pain, nothing else. To my amazement through the years, I have had several mediums ask me if I saved my husband's life. I smile and say I tried hard but there was a different path for him. Denny felt guilty for losing a friend on a plane that crashed. He was supposed to be on that plane, they switched flights that day. I used to tell him it was not his time to go and to stop blaming himself. Sometimes Wes (the person he switched flights with) will come in during medium demonstration with Denny. Denny used to make me all kinds of music tapes. This was his way of telling me how he felt. Even though Danny passed many years ago, I still get his messages through music, and it makes me smile and feel his love.

## Chapter 7

## Saturn Returns

*"A person who never made a mistake, never tried anything new."* Albert Einstein

Saturn returns. You're probably wondering what that means. When I was going through my first Saturn return, I had absolutely no idea, nor had I ever heard about it. Here is a definition of what it is and means. In horoscopic astrology, a Saturn return is an astrological transit that occurs when the planet Saturn returns to the same place in the sky that it occupied at the moment of a person's birth. Every 27-29 years you will have a Saturn return. The planet Saturn is the taskmaster of the zodiac. It also happens to be the ruler of my sun sign Capricorn. I was always interested in looking in the daily newspaper or a magazine for my horoscope not realizing it was just a general sign horoscope and that it may hit, or it may not. Have you engaged in this activity and find it fun, intriguing, and mysterious? Astrology is a concept with many levels. I love looking at it now, but from a different perspective than when I was younger and had no knowledge other than what my sun sign is.

Back then, I was too naïve to understand it. I copied this description from an astrology site as I really love their descriptions. This is from the website: *https://astrostyle.com/saturn-return/* put out by Horoscopes by the Astrotwins. In astrological lore, Saturn is the great taskmaster of the skies. We prefer the term life coach or personal trainer since Saturn is "cruel" to be kind. It breaks you down, makes you lift the heavy weights so you can build those rock-hard muscles and get into fighting shape! Wherever Saturn is in your chart, it always points to your toughest lessons, the ones you might become obsessed with breaking through. We often see people finding careers that match the zodiac sign their Saturn is in. It is not surprising since Saturn can help us with excellence and mastery. Here is where we will toil away for hours, obsessively, to reach our grandest goals. It makes sense that Saturn is the ruler of ambitious Capricorn, the high-achieving, hardest working kid in the zodiac. (Cosmic fact: Saturn is cycling through its home sign of Capricorn from December 19, 2017 to March 21, 2020.)

During the Saturn return—which lasts 2.5 to 3 years you will come face to face with your own blocks and be forced to push through them. All the "mistakes" you made in the nearly three decades leading up to this seem to crystallize. Rather than repeating them on autopilot, you have a chance to turn lemons into lemonade. And if you refuse to heed those lessons, Saturn will bring a drill sergeant style smackdown. Indeed, the Saturn return starts off feeling a bit like boot camp for a lot of people. But drop and give him twenty instead of rebelling against those barking orders. Three years later, you will be General Awesome or Captain Fantastic of your own kick-ass army at the very least, you will be decorated with a star or two.

Some of you reading this may be in this phase, or are now looking back at your life during that time, and remembering what you personally experienced. I am not an astrologer; I have many friends that are, and I have learned enough through them and consider myself dangerous on the subject. This is just an example of what happened for me during this first Saturn Return. Now I want you to think about these times in your life and what was happening for you. My husband was killed at 28 years of age and I was 27. We were both in our first Saturn return. I became a single mother in the blink of an eye. I had mentioned earlier that he and I had met his detailer for transfer information. The day of Denny's funeral I found out he was accepted for Officer Candidate school and he got his east coast transfer. Had he left the four wheeling alone, he would have lived to see more advancement in his career and may still be with us here today. The taskmaster set him on a task for advancement, yet it also set him on a task for risky behavior.

I decided to return to Maine and go back to where I had

worked before. It was not long before I was promoted in my work. I received that promotion because I had high work standards and was dependable. An employer's dream in today's world. I put my nose to the grindstone at work and took care of my young son. I began to date, but not many survived my antenna or grief state. One of whom I met about a year and half after Denny passed. We had this off and on thing which was driven by me knowing stuff. I would feel it and of course I found out I was right about him having a girlfriend back home. So I would tell him no on seeing him. He would always show back up telling me he was confused about who he wanted to be with. That went on until he got me pregnant and then he disappeared, denying it. I lost a husband at 27 and gave birth to my second child at 30. I was told after I had my first son it was highly unlikely I would ever have any more children. I tended to believe that since my kids are seven years apart. That is until I was told I was pregnant again!

I thought I went through hell with death, now I would go through hell with life. The people who wanted me to get rid of my son were just hurtful and mean spirited. His father put me through the ringer on paternity. There is no denying DNA, and God has a sense of humor as my son looks just like his father. Not only was my pregnancy hurtful emotionally, the birth almost took my life. Thank God for good friends and family though, as they got me through it. I looked over at my mother and I could read in her eyes that she was scared to death. She really believed I was going to die. I asked the nurses to take her out of the birthing room until it was over. My good friend Pam stayed with me. I did not think I would make it some days after the birth of my youngest. I had to return to work after only five weeks of giving birth.

Now this is how the taskmaster manifests in our lives and pushes us to make needed changes. Think back to this time and look at what happened and how you grew or maybe you are going through this now. The key is to stay focused and do not give up on yourself. Look at the list of these wonderful talented gifted people who made risky choices and were taken out by the taskmaster. Janis Joplin 27, Jimi Hendrix 27, Amy Winehouse 27, Kurt Cobain 27, Jim Morrison 27, Heath Ledger 29, Brandon Lee 28 are just some. During this time frame we are stretched to the max for growth. We have so many wonderful natural stages of life and our first Saturn return is to mature and grow our inner selves. At this stage for me, I was a maiden and mother, now I am the crone. The journey for me was, my maiden and mother collided in time. The maiden is the planning stages of our dreams and hopes about what we would like to see in our lives. This phase is not that grounded yet as you can see. The mother phase is the doing phase, setting up our foundations to survive and thrive in the world around us.

Because we are all individuals, this is not always done the same. We do it by the trial and error of what works in our lives that keeps us moving forward. I was on my knees many nights praying for both of my sons during this period in their lives. I talked a lot to spirits and angels. In fact, it was during my oldest son's Saturn that a huge angel appeared in my room at night. I had always felt them, this was the first time I saw one. It took up the whole corner of my room right up to the ceiling, this light being. Some of my friends who are fellow empaths, psychics and mediums will call these light beings Aliens. I did not, however, feel invaded. I felt calmed, so for me it was angelic. This phase we go through can be intense for empaths. We are the feelers of the world, the canaries that go out and test the energy for whether it's toxic or safe. I have completed two Saturn returns and now I have Saturn on my sun sign. Lots of things are happening.

Your second Saturn return is the assimilating of all the knowledge you have amassed on the second leg of your journey. We come to terms within ourselves, the true teachings of our lives, what have we become, and who we truly are. This is the crone stage. The second Saturn return is at age 58-60. Anything that has set us back, family dynamics, personal relationships, etc., we decide what to keep and what to let go of at this point. This period can be difficult for some as we are moved to leave the maiden and mother in us behind, to become the teacher, the wisdom, the crone. No matter where you personally are at this stage, you can see the importance of these life phases. Look at where you are personally and use that as your guide. I have learned from this process that spirit, God, and the Universe are really in charge. They bring us choices. We will look at the path, and by our choices it is that path we experience in life. How many times have you heard someone say it is their free will, or you can lead a horse to water, but you cannot make them drink? Wise sayings. We learn to detach from that which causes unrest as it forces us to look at truths in a grounded practical way. This phase shows us our own mortality and our vulnerabilities. This period of detachment is one of the key functions of the second Saturn return. I have been talking about this book for the last decade. The purpose is to share my wisdom and experiences, and possibly help those along the way that struggle with being an empath, intuitive and medium. Some days the energy of this can become so heavy, it's important at this time, above all else, to take care of yourselves. You can burn out with stress and not even realize that you are literally carrying the weight of the world up on your shoulders. Learning how to let go of others' pain and worry so that you can thrive and grow is key. This is more challenging for some; we think we are abandoning, yet we are not. The urge to fix and mother everything that is broken needs to be put into perspective. By our second Saturn return, we should be in full bloom with all the projects that we have been working on in our lives as they start to bear fruit. We have also let go of those dreams we may have thought we wanted and defined what we will keep. It is important to always remember that it is the job of the student to seek out the teacher. It is the teacher's job to be prepared for the moment the student arrives. It is my intention to make sense of the things in life that may become confusing. It is common to over analyze and forget to go with the flow of the tide and not go against it. We can make the lessons that we learn, even the tough ones, more palatable by the way we choose, react, and move forward. Now that you have learned that Saturn is the great teacher and task master, thank Saturn for the lessons it has taught you, and for pushing you to grow in so many ways beyond your conscious dreams.

# Chapter 8

## Just Knowing

Have you ever found yourself just knowing about something you have no way of knowing? I know that sounds crazy in the written words, yet those of you who understand what is written here understand exactly what I mean. It is just, knowing that seems to come out of thin air. I remember family members wanting me to leave a certain job that I had. I stood my ground and said, "this job is temporary and I will become management, you just watch." Well, they did not believe me. They could not see what I knew, and I was right. Sadly though, one of them did not live to see it happen, but the others did. I have found that when I trust my intuition and just step into what I know, I can manifest whatever it is with focus and confidence. Did I say confidence? Yes, I did! The knowing just gives one the sense that everything will be fine. When I work with my clients, whether it be life coaching, readings, or hypnosis, I tap into their knowing. This is the thread that I always follow. It is your truth that is known to you without knowing how you know, you just do.

Connecting to our higher selves takes time to learn - how to get out of our own way. One of the hardest things an empath needs to understand is that we have this uncanny ability to see what a person can become, or what I call their; soul energy. We can get pulled into that side of the person and ignore what they are doing with their behaviors. When I get a feeling about someone or something, I pay attention. Mothers just know when something is off with their kids, spouses notice each other, and family members tune in too. Have you ever met a stranger and get the overwhelming feeling that you must get away from that person, or even a place? It is just something you know; you are logically not seeing anything in the lower world, yet your higher self has that knowing.

When we lived in Italy, my 13-year-old son came home begging to adopt this street puppy. I said no. I just knew that there was something not right. I said we do not know what this puppy may have. We were new to Italy and he was having a hard time adjusting to a new home, new country, new school etc. I broke down about the sixth time he begged me. She was a beautiful puppy, half Shepherd and Doberman. We named her Ebony. Within the first week she came down with Parvo. But between the hospital and the home care, we got her through it. Before we could get her shots, she got distemper. We no sooner got that little fighter through the distemper, and then it was tick fever! Nine months of keeping this little girl alive and a lot of money. Whenever we walked her, everyone would say what a beautiful dog she was. Sadly though, after all that, she was stolen from our fenced yard. I was heartbroken, as were the kids. She was thrown out on the streets and then stolen after we loved, healed, trained, and grew her. I knew there was heartbreak with that puppy, I just did not have all the details. I am sure you can think of a time when you had knowledge about something but did it anyway. I was sad because she was taken, yet I was happy that she found us, otherwise she would have never survived. I know in my heart that she made some family happy. There were several kids in our area and most of them really liked her. We never found out who took her though. I feel that wherever she went she was ok, so I was able to let go and move on. That is, until I took on two more dogs off the streets. A Belgian Malinois Shepherd and a white Shepherd. These were two beautiful dogs. The white one was female. I named her Bonnie. The male I named Clyde. Bonnie fooled me though. She was going to have puppies. She must have hooked up with a black lab as the puppies all had web paws, and they were all black. So now it was a new dog adventure. Clyde adopted me;, he was left by a US service member on the streets of Italy. He was huge when he came running up to me, I froze. I petted his head, he followed me to my car. I said goodbye doggie and I got in my car to drive home. I heard this God-awful noise and I looked at my boyfriend in the car and I said "wow, what is that?" He looked at me and said it was the dog running after the car crying! I looked in the rearview mirror and at once pulled off the road. I opened my car door and in the back he jumped. I said "well, I hope they get along." I had just adopted Bonnie the day before. Clyde was so happy to be with me. That dog would know when I left the base to drive home. He would wait at the door until I got home. He found me and would not take no for an answer. When he first started running towards me, I did not know what to do and I thought "I hope he does not bite, that is one big dog!" It was like he knew me already and that is just the way it went. Whenever I went into the US for conferences, I had to call home and talk to him on the phone so he would eat. That dog was stuck to me like glue and no one was coming in the yard without his permission. He kept us safe. Let me tell you, no one was going to try and steal him. So, we saved Ebony, Bonnie, Clyde, and Bonnie's 7 babies from the streets of Italy. They, in return, protected the house from invasion. Bonnie went to a good friend's house in Sicily after she had a home invasion. I kept Clyde and found homes for all the babies; one was brought back because their other dog wanted to kill it. It all worked out. Clyde just knew that I would take him if he showed me, he was a good boy. I miss my dogs now, I just have the cats.

Now, how many of you have ever just known that your significant other was stepping out without any actual proof? It was something you just knew. Men that cheat do not stand a chance with me. I will know and will catch them at it. I just get shown and then boom, there it is. Have you ever found yourself in that situation? Then, you sometimes wish you never knew! And why do you just know? It can be frustrating and freeing all at the same time. This ability can also hinder you from trusting if you get in your head, and that will hold you back from seeking a great partner. It is a fine line, and we must allow our partner, and ourselves, to explore with an open mind and have the ability to tap into truth. How about when your child brings home a friend you just know is going to be trouble for your child? How about siblings, parents, or friends that you are close to? It is a fine line, and you want to encourage healthy relationships for them, yet that person is not sitting right with you. Sometimes you can warn them, and other times they must learn for themselves. The natural guardian comes out in you. There have been many times I wish that I had been wrong. We are here in the school of life, and we are all on our own path.

Being a good listener and emotional support is sometimes all that you may be able to do with some of those situations. There are some things for some people that must be experienced in harsh ways to learn. Sad as it is to say, it is the balance of life, the yin and yang. Without the sadness we would not know what happiness is. I learned at a very young age to be grateful and that I was not a victim; if I did the work, I could change my current struggles into the motivation to strive for a better life. I knew this in my heart without being told. It is the old soul in me. I would drive my mother nuts with some of the things I would just decide to do. What becomes hard for empaths is knowing when to let go. We are a light to those in the dark. Narcissists seem to seek us out. They have a knowledge of our good hearts. Takers are drawn to givers. I know you have seen good people getting taken advantage of and having so many struggles in life because they continually give to others but starve themselves. This is one of the major things' empaths must learn to do. Take care of your needs, recharge your batteries, it is ok to say no. No can mean not at this moment, it does not have to mean no forever.

It is your right to receive all the blessings this life has to offer too. There has been this misconception that anyone who is spiritual or religious should work for free. I can tell you that if all their needs were met and they were taken care of in healthy living conditions and in harmony with nature most of them would be more than happy to. Yet that is not a reality for most. We have bills to pay just like everyone else does. Our work is exhausting and many days so sad you may find yourself crying to release the energy. Those of us who walk in this path carry a lot of responsibility for being a loving light to help others see what they can manifest. I have always been, in some form or another, in the service to others. Many of us have similarities in this process and others are completely different. I cannot say this enough - there is only one of you, you are an individual no matter how many want to try and put you in a certain box. If you live in your truth and be true to yourself, you can have a good life. I will tell people when I do readings, I will give you what I see. I will always be kind in my delivery, yet I must stick to what I get. After all, I want to be the best service to you and I always want to feel that I am honoring the truth no matter how hard it could be. When we can look at problems through truthful kind eyes, then we can make the best solutions for ourselves with kindness too.

Life can be hard, just as nature can be brutal. We must learn to flow like the river, bend like the tree and know that every storm has an end, and the sunshine comes. Sometimes it takes a while to get where you are headed, after all, it is in God's time for us in the end. There is one thing that I am sure of. Our soul never dies, our spirit lives on. Knowing this really calms any preconceived notions of the cycle of life. We will all leave our physical bodies someday just to shine in another. The next time you start to question yourself about just knowing, stop and listen. This could have been a really bad thing for me if I had not listened. I was staying at a hotel I had never been to before in Vegas. I was attending a conference. I left my room and headed towards the elevator. The door opened and I saw a man standing inside by himself. The hair rose all over my body and I saw it in his eyes. I looked directly at him and said, "oh my, I forgot something in my room" and I bolted back to my room. This man came out of the elevator and proceeded to have a complete mental breakdown. I could hear him from my room while I was dialing hotel security. If I had gotten in that elevator with him, I may not be here writing this. What I am describing to you is not paranoia it is just a known that comes out of the blue.

Pay attention to your lightning bolts and see what emerges. Learning to listen to your inner knowing, your body, mind and spirit will keep you in a good place. I remember one morning getting up noticing in the mirror I had this rash, and it was itching and burning. I thought at first it looked like an allergic reaction. I watched it that day. The next morning the minute my foot hit the floor I heard in my head you have the shingles. I got myself dressed and headed to the walk-in clinic and when the doctor came in and verified that I was right. He asked me when the rash appeared, I told him and, luckily, I was in the 72-hour window and got an antiviral. The same thing happened to me with my thyroid condition. I was misdiagnosed and suffered for over seven years with it. I knew what it was, but blood tests did not show it, so the doctors told me it was not that. It most certainly was exactly what I had said it was. Pay attention to your inner knowing, it can save your life.

## CHAPTER 9

## THE DRAGONFLY

Have you ever realized that, in life, if everything stays the same it never truly grows? Growth comes from taking those leaps of faith in life and allowing yourself to take the chance to make things more exciting, better, or just adventurous. There are so many cliches about this in life. Like the seven-year itch, wanting to stretch and grow. If things get complacent and go on longer than they should, the universe steps in to help you make those shifts. Some of them can be explosive and life altering! The name of this chapter gives meaning to just that. Dragonflies signify transformation in your life. It awakens the passion within you to do what feels right for you. This is the time when the magic and mystery in your life is awakening. It goes beyond simple change. It is a total transformation of your life. These little gems are part of the elementals and fairy realm. I know you may be thinking; what is that? Elementals are part of our beautiful planet and nature, and the fairies are just little magical beings of energy. Have you ever got a glimpse or caught something out of the corner of your eye while in a nature setting or garden? If that answer is yes, you more than likely saw a fairy.

This leads me to another story of my growth and what got me to do the work I do know and love so much. I was living in Southern California working for the Department of Defense. I had moved across the country to take a new position. What a change and a shift was coming into my life! When it is time to step into this work, if you are not going in willingly, and throw caution to the wind, it will create a storm like no other in your life. I had been a DOD employee for over 20 years with an outstanding service record. I made the move from the east coast to the west coast in January of 2004. I had just gone through a major health issue that sent me back to the US from overseas in 2001. I was on the mend once I was diagnosed with what my intuition had already told me it was. A reminder; if you are not feeling well and you just know something is off, follow through until you get answers and always get a second or even a third opinion. You must be your own health advocate. On to the story. I have always been that girl, that woman that seems to just get baptized by fire no matter what it is when change is occurring. Luckily, it could be the luck of the Irish or that I am like the chameleon and able to blend into whatever the environment is, either way it has made me a survivor.

When I first arrived, I had a major renovation of a building under way and my bosses had ultimate trust in my ability to oversee this operation. I did not disappoint. My one boss from the Region was getting ready to retire and her replacement was sent all around to the different bases to meet all the department heads. When this man came to my office to meet me and I shook his hand the hair stood up on my arms and the back of my neck and I knew I was in for it. I will not go into the horror story that unfolded over the next two years of my life. I will say this, I stood my ground, went out on my terms and stepped into where I was meant to be. Even though this man was the most hateful, mean spirited, envious, sick individual, had it not been for him I would have continued where I was, not growing, just barely staying above water. My first clue to get out was my health. What I was shown made me physically and emotionally sick; how good people in government are walked on and treated like trash.

After a brief retreat back to Maine, I realized it was no longer the place for me, so I returned to California. Upon returning to the west coast, I threw myself into my spiritual growth, and enrolled in the Hypnosis college in Tarzana, Ca. Although I had used my intuition in my work my whole life and delved into what I called a hobby of readings, I had now I started making a living at it. I immersed myself into learning day and night while doing readings for clients. When I first started readings, I used Tarot. I love these cards and the beauty of the many different decks. I have quite a collection of them. I have one deck that is just about falling apart. This is the one I started using for paid clients. About six months into my regular readings, I started noticing a shift within myself. I was not quite sure what was happening, but I just went with it. For some strange reason, several of my regular clients and I would start sneezing during readings. This would only happen with certain people, and it would continue. It was so annoying. It got so bad that some of them started to ask if I was allergic to them. It was really starting to get to me.

I decided to take a few days off from readings to clear, ground and center myself. While I was out in my yard, I was tending to my little herb garden and a hummingbird came right nose to nose with me and I heard it; "The sneezing will stop when you listen to spirit!" Now, of course, I am like "ok, just what does that mean?" As I explained in a previous chapter my connection to the animal kingdom was strong as a child, now it was flooding back into my life. My guide is native, he sends me to the animal kingdom when I am searching for answers. Here was this soft, gentle little bird in my face, humming the words to my mind. I learned to be more flexible with my growth in the coming days.

After my little messenger departed, I went on with my day. I went to sleep that evening reminiscing about what had happened that day. The next morning, as I was sitting out on my patio drinking coffee, I was watching all the butterflies in my wildflower bed and it hit me like a ton of bricks! Butterflies come out of a cocoon and emerge in an array of bold colors into life. They also represent the spirit realm. The reason I was sneezing with certain people was because spirit was trying desperately to get my attention, and I was not listening. They do have a sense of humor. I think they say to themselves or each other "Let us get so obnoxious so she will have to pay attention." Bingo, the lights went on, and from that day forward if I start sneezing during a reading that is not connected to mediumship reading, I stop and say I have a spirit here that wants to emerge. Do you want me to continue or would you like to see what that spirit wants to say? If they say no, I move on and the sneezing stops once I acknowledge spirit is there.

How cool is that. It took six months of sneezing repeatedly with certain people for me to say UNCLE, I give. I started to feel a tapping like sensation on my head. It got to be intense and annoying until finally one day I said "hey, if you must be doing that could you be a little gentle please?" Guess what? The tapping got lighter. When they felt they had achieved the opening of my crown to their satisfaction, it finally stopped. I was relieved to say the least.

Now here I go with what I never wanted to do, and guess what that was? Yep, the mediumship. There were many reasons that I did not desire to go down that road at that time, but my life was going to change in many ways as I was learning and growing fast. I had to for survival.

Now I do it all. Yet, like anything that you do, the more you practice an art the more fine-tuned you become.

One of my mentors, John Holland, told me all mediums are psychic but not all psychics are mediums. I have learned so much from his teachings. He continues to amaze me to this day. Watching a live demonstration with him is like watching a fine-tuned orchestra as he connects with the spirits of loved ones passed.

I must also mention another person I consider one of my mentors, a local psychic that helped me to grow on many levels, and fine tune my abilities. She was drawn to me in a public setting just five months after my husband had passed. She introduced herself and revealed enough about what she saw going on around me, that I decided to go and see her privately. She felt my sadness and broken heart. And from that point on, I was a client. Soon we became close friends. We have had lives together, and we continue to be an important part of each other's lives. She lives in the Mid-Coast Maine area and her name is Brenda Hanna.

I have studied with many different types of settings and beliefs and it greatly enhances my growth. Though there may be vast differences, I choose what resonates with my energy. One of the most important aspects of your journey here in the physical is to be true to yourself and your calling. As I have expressed previously, there is only one you, you are an individual and you are not anyone else.

You are your unique self. Be genuine and truthful to your own spirit and things will flow in the direction that they are meant to. You know that old saying "when the student is ready the teacher will show up!" So, wax on wax off grasshopper! (For those of you who may not know what that means, it's from the movie Karate Kid from in the 80's.)

My business started to explode. I was busy with readings. I was at the end of attending the Hypnosis School and getting ready to graduate. It was a blessing to have that turn around in my life. At one point I thought "if this does not shift soon on the financial side, I could become homeless." It was a blessing to finally start to see the rewards from the risk that I took on my future. My ability became a success, making way for me to step into where I was supposed to be. At this point in time, I was growing, spiritually, at a very fast pace. I still had the naysayers, the poo poos, but did I allow that to affect me? Nope, not in the least. Some of them were even family members, but I did not let them get me down. I had been told before that I couldn't do this, or don't do that, but the person telling this could not see what I could see. I did not hold it against them, I just focused on my goal. No one else walks in your shoes but you, make sure they fit you and feel right for you. We only get one go-around in this lifetime, so live it for you, not how others think you should be living. Having told you my stories, I am sure you have your own unique stories of your connection to your higher self. There is a process to silence the noise of the critical thinking mind. For me it includes getting rest, eating right, walking in nature, meditating, clearing out old energy, going into a state of trance, turning off electronics and just tuning in and leaving the chattering world to itself. Music is so soothing; it really calms the mind. Just leave the heavy metal head banging out. Music does influence us, and it can be positive or negative, so choose wisely. It is also very healing. I have heard the angelic choir and there is nothing else like it, it's so hard to even describe. As I end this chapter remember to give yourself permission to recharge your own life energy. For me, I must recharge to be of service to others in need. Love starts with you and in you.

# Chapter 10

## 2020 Vision

What a year for the books this has been. Total shock and awe of our way of life. My good friend in southern California called me a few months back and said to me "when you foresaw this many years ago, I thought maybe you were just dreaming, or out of your mind! You were right on with people dropping like flies across the globe." I was unable to see what caused it, only that it came out of the blue and caused massive damage. This is the year that has rocked our very foundations, our core energy. 2020 represents clear vision, being able to see what has been hidden. Have you ever wondered why evil people get away with things over and over, or that bullies keep pushing people around and nothing seems to change? It can be disheartening to say the least. God always has a plan. When we get complacent and allow that behavior to enter our societies, we ourselves create monsters much like a parent spoils a child so much that no one can stand to be around them. We have now come to that point where massive corruption is commonplace in our country and the world. We have come to a big reckoning of truths being put in front of us. Fear (false evidence appearing real); Will we run, or will we rise and face it? I say we face it! We are so torn apart by the mass hysteria, and media hypnosis! And yes, I did say that. We are watching our very own government do to its people what abusers do to their victims. Where criminals become victims and victims become criminals. How do we save our world as we know it? By standing together. Do not let them divide us by race, religion, skin color or parties. Back in 2010 I wrote a blog for a company that I am an independent contractor of. Due to contractual conditions, I am not allowed to tell you who or what it is, but I will tell you they are global and well known. I quit writing blogs for this company because my writings would become their property. I will give you an overview of what was written:

I wrote about the ascension to the age of Aquarius how it was occurring back at that time during the process of that moment in time. We were having major earth changes, or shifts causing movement of the earth at very deep levels. As a result, we experienced more of the higher vibrations. Mother Earth was restructuring herself – she was realigning to receive these new and higher frequencies, as she still is to this day. Some people will call this climate change. But it is the earth change that is happening, the same way every planet in the universe has gone through changes for eons. At the same time, everything in the universe is realigning as well. We were feeling the first ripples of the major changes. We started a new earth, or 'Earth Two." While Mother Earth and the universe realign, we do too. We are all connected. Body aches and various pains may be present. For me personally, it's feeling dizzy and enduring headaches. Sweating and hot flashes are occurring for many because we are burning off any lower vibrational energy within each one of us as we adjust. When you have lower vibrating thoughts, or any thoughts of fear or negativity that cannot exist in this reality, you may immediately become excruciatingly hot and begin to sweat. Be aware these hot flashes and sweats are not all hormonal – this serves as to help with our own alignment tools.

With the intensity of energy inhabiting the earth recently, we may feel as though we are hyperventilating and cannot sit still. During this time, take the time to meditate, listen to music that is calming and go on a no news diet for a few days. You will be amazed at how good that can feel. I spoke earlier about the ascension to the age of Aquarius; we have been growing more and more towards the **Harmonic Convergence.** The Harmonic Convergence is the name given to the world's first synchronized global peace meditation, which occurred on August 16–17, 8024Bc. This event will also happen again on the august 16-17, 2024.**Wikipedia**

Now I will add a quote from a book that is a great read about conversations with two entities the author called ascended masters. I feel this quote is so very synchronistic in today's world that leaving it out would be a great injustice. The author's name is Gary R Renard, his book is titled: The Disappearance of the Universe. This is a conversation that Gary had with one of the masters. It went like this.

Gary: *"This correction you speak of, does it have anything to do with Political correctness?"*

Pursha: *"No. Political correctness, no matter how well the intentioned, is still an attack on the freedom of speech. You will find we are very free with our speech indeed. The word correction is not used by us in the usual way, because to correct something usually means to fix it up and keep it. When the false universe is finished being corrected by the Holy Spirit, it will no longer appear to exist."*

Look at what we are witnessing in our world today: a global virus, global shutdowns that have closed business across the world. We have a fight going on in the consciousness of man. What will we choose? Will we choose the light or the dark? Our world has been out of balance for so long now that we are having to work in tandem towards alignment with ourselves and God and alignment with community and humanity. Thanksgiving has just passed, and I am grateful for all the blessings in my life. There are planetary line-ups that have not occurred in over 4000 years as we continue to move towards the age of Aquarius. Right after Thanksgiving we entered what is called by astrologers a stellium (a cluster of three or more planets in the same sign or house) of **Jupiter/ Saturn/Pluto** in Capricorn over the weekend. There is a shift of major proportions. We are moving towards Christmas and the ending of another decade. Here is what this stellium means in layman's terms. Lucky for me, I have a lot of astrologer friends that share with me the information about these things very deeply. Triple conjunction means:

**Jupiter** – Justice, Expansion, Wisdom, Joy, & Gratitude

**Saturn** – Being a Grown up, Responsible, Responsive with Maturity

**Pluto** – Uncovering and Purging the Shadow of Lies and deceit. What is hidden creates Empowerment as we move into Truth

We are truly stepping towards the age of Aquarius as we zig zag through the steps needed for the realignment of humanity. Our earth is realigning and evolving and so are we. There is a saying that is so relevant, even though we may not like it; The truth will set you free, and allow you to make the best decisions for your highest and best good, even if it is shocking and goes against what you thought before you knew what you did not know.

No matter the outcome of what is coming to light, I believe in my heart that God has a plan for us all. There are so many people praying in this world right now that I know when it blows like a hurricane, it will level the playing field for the divine to shine just like the sun will enter once the storm has passed. Without dark we do not appreciate light, without sadness we do not appreciate joy. Without work and focus we do not appreciate the success of our soul's journey and what each one of us came here to do. We do create our reality and choose which one we want to live in. It is our God given right to choose. We are going to show all the ugly truths. Will we rise and step into change, or will we freeze and give up? I have faith that we will rise, even though the deep-seated beliefs of cognitive dissonance in some is that we must overcome to be able to move forward. This belief is deep seeded so strongly in some people, that when the truth is presented, they are unable to accept it. Their minds conflict with the evidence so greatly that they cannot accept it as the truth. Only once the truth comes out can we move forward with resolutions to conflict. What a major shift that has touched all of us to our core at one level or another. All this pain and uncomfortable energy was necessary for us to see the truth more clearly. The year is not over yet and so much more is being brought to light. We have been led to believe things that are just not true, and things that are true being reported as false. Stay strong! We will make it! Our heavenly father is in charge. "The lord is my light and my salvation; whom shall I fear? The lord is the strength of my life; of whom shall I be afraid?" - Psalms 27:1

I trust with my heart and soul that we will heal this nation and be a light to help heal others as we let go of the title of human trafficking and crimes against our own people by the corrupt in all areas of our societies. We are now adjusting our vision and can see clearly that 2020 will be a year we will never forget.

# Chapter 11

# Vibrational Destination

Today, as I write this chapter, is the last day of the eleventh month of a decade with a lunar eclipse in Gemini. Like I said, I am not an astrologer, but the moon energy and clearing that is about to happen will be monumental. Lunar eclipses are course correctors and mercury rules Gemini and the mind. Media will be affected by this in a big way. There will be so many secrets and things hidden coming out where the media is concerned. Communication will be busy with new facts as they shine to light, this will be felt throughout the world. What has been hidden will become indisputable and those that have been fooled with deception will awaken to the truth no matter how hard this will be it will set the world free. We will let go of the overthinking; we will start to intuit the higher self of our life. Our minds cannot give us wisdom from within; only when we tune in will we be able to see the truth of the vibrational destination of God, truth, balance, justice and love that lives within all of us.

We must face the duality that resides within us. Stay

connected to the God energy that resides within you. Thoughts are not feelings; these are logical mind experiences that we have gone through. Thoughts are not always the truth; they are things that may have happened in the past that may not be relevant in the now. Our thoughts are great in the way they help navigate logical common sense practical experiences. When we feel in our lives, we can get in touch with our own essence of who we are at the very soul level. What we are experiencing is a deep level of tuning in to our own selves and seeing the truth in things no matter what we use to think. You have heard the saying thoughts become things, they do if we let them rule our minds and we focus on them. Words spoken can be like knives and cut you to your core if you let them. Do not let others words affect you so much that you begin to believe projections or lies about yourself or others.

In your mind and soul say to yourself, "I do not accept that lower vibrational energy that you are sending my way." If allowed, those words will affect you in negative ways. They begin controlling you, which is totally against an empath's nature of freedom. We begin manifesting some of the very things we fear. Do not invest in the negativity. I love this old Native saying and it is so true, now more than ever in these Orwellian times of tribulation where we have disconnected from humanity.

Words are just words and they cannot hurt you unless you allow them to. Remember the old saying: "sticks and stones may break my bones, but words will never hurt me?" This is the very reason it is so important to unplug, listen to soothing, healing music, get out in nature, and listen to what Mother Earth (Gaia) is saying to us on a deeper level. Our vibrational level has been changing on a deep level and now we are at the point of a major shift. I love this native story about the two wolves.

*ONE EVENING, AN ELDERLY CHEROKEE BRAVE TOLD HIS GRANDSON ABOUT A BATTLE THAT*

*GOES ON INSIDE PEOPLE. HE SAID, "MY SON, THE BATTLE IS BETWEEN TWO 'WOLVES' INSIDE US ALL. ONE IS EVIL. IT IS ANGER, ENVY, JEALOUSY, SORROW, REGRET, GREED, ARROGANCE, SELF-PITY, GUILT, RESENTMENT, INFERIORITY, LIES, FALSE PRIDE, SUPERIORITY, AND EGO.*

*THE OTHER IS GOOD. IT IS JOY, PEACE, LOVE, HOPE, SERENITY, HUMILITY, KINDNESS, BENEVOLENCE, EMPATHY, GENEROSITY, TRUTH, COMPASSION, AND FAITH."*

*THE GRANDSON THOUGHT ABOUT IT FOR A MINUTE AND THEN ASKED HIS GRANDFATHER: "WHICH WOLF WINS?..."*

*THE OLD CHEROKEE SIMPLY REPLIED, "THE ONE THAT YOU FEED THE MOST"*

Use your mind, do not let it use you. Our minds are

powerful. Yet without connecting all these things together for true inner peace, we will wander endlessly seeking and searching. Connecting all three: mind, body and spirit, is our true wealth and health here on earth. This is the Trinity of the Holy Spirit. Thanking our creator, being grateful for blessings, and being kind to others will bring peace and serenity into your life like no other. This brings us all full circle to our vibrational destinations. It takes practice to tune into the vibrations around you, and once you make that connection and start feeling it, it will always be there to guide you. Everything has vibrational energy in the universe: people, animals, music, the earth, flowers, you name it. Have you ever seen an aura without looking for one and just noticed it? It is fascinating to do. If you are looking at an object, person, or animal against a solid background you will see it if you just look above the person's or object's head. A white background is best for this.

 I was sitting with a group of mediums at the Edgar Cayce Foundation last November listening to John Holland and Janet Nohavec speak. I soon noticed, without looking, that they both were emanating this huge aura around each other. It was amazing to witness as I watched it merge as they spoke about many different aspects of mediumship. I so enjoyed my time at the foundation and I really connected with it vibrationally, and I knew it immediately. While I was there, of course I was going to take some of the Cayce Foundation Spa Treatments. The spa area is located in the old building where this all began. As I walked down a hall to get to the room, I started to feel dizzy and lightheaded. I mentioned it to the young woman who was about to do my treatment. She thought maybe I was just dehydrated. I finished the first treatment and then was taken to another room. As I continued down the hall, I came upon a woman with the biggest smile, standing in a doorway waiting for me. Her name was Aurora. She gave me a big hug and welcomed me into the space she has been doing treatments in for over 30 years. I said to her that I was very lightheaded and felt dizzy. She smiled at me and said "it's because you are one of us. You are feeling the vortex in the facility today." While I got my treatment, she told me wonderful stories about the foundation. She also told me that the vortex moves to different areas and that it just so happened to be in the spa area at that time.

You may wonder just who this Edgar Cayce is. I have added this directly from the foundation's website:

**About Edgar Cayce**

Edgar Cayce (1877-1945) has been called the "sleeping prophet," the "father of holistic medicine," and the most documented psychic of the 20th century. Cayce was born on a farm in Hopkinsville, Kentucky, in 1877, and his psychic abilities began to appear as early as his childhood. As an adult, Cayce would put himself into a state of meditation, connecting with the universal consciousness and from this state, came his "readings". From holistic health and the treatment of illness to dream interpretation and reincarnation, Cayce's readings and insights offer practical help and advice to individuals from all walks of life, even today.

I personally have been very blessed by my teachers and those of my tribe in this time of major world shifts. Things just seem to connect when it's time to do so. I am also amid a vibrational shift and change of my own new vibrational destination. I have come out of the shadows so to speak. I now speak my truth even though there are others who may not understand. With my clients there is no judgement, only healing universal love. I am honest, not brutal. We have all had our walks in life and our paths seem to cross because of the vibrational connection at that time in space. I am grateful and humbled that they choose to connect with me for whatever healing, coaching, readings, or entertainment needs that they may be seeking.

As we progress through the rest of December 2020, the eclipse energy along with the solstice on Dec 21, 2020 will result in a huge burst of truth, connection, and Christ consciousness. You may feel like resting up as we come to the end of the tumultuous year that has affected the world. There will be more and more light workers appearing to assist all of those who have been blinded purposely by corrupt entities and media. They will no longer be able to hide the crimes against humanity. I would like you to give this a test and see how it works for you. Do not give up; practice until you see it. Have a friend or set a plant or animal up against a white backdrop. Now just focus above the head and keep staring there. Now, as you continue to practice this you will begin to see the auric field of the person or object rising, this is their aura or energy. I love it when I get colors.

There are so many things that the naked eye cannot see and things we can see if we look beyond, we all have our own vibrational frequency just like our fingerprints. Can we shift our energy? Yes, we can, and it changes as we grow and learn over time. Have you ever had an aura photo done with the special camera? I do them yearly if I am able to. Without fail, whatever is going on in my life that is affecting my energy, will show in the colors of the photos. Those photos you can usually get taken at Holistic Fairs if you are curious to see yours. They will come with their meaning of the colors in the aura photo. Speaking of photos, this summer I got some activity on my camera with energy orbs on my deck. I have saved them and will post a video on my website. I have been lucky to get these types of photos, so I think I will start a new hobby of visiting sites that have energy spots or spiritual activity still active and take some photos.

Have you ever noticed that certain people around you just drain you? I call them energy suckers; they just drain you dry of life force energy. It is important for sensitives and empaths to protect themselves from this even if its family members who do this. It throws you off balance and disturbs your peace. The biggest lesson a sensitive or empath needs to learn is that it is ok to say "no." Actually, if you want to survive, you need to learn that not everyone that comes your way will accept your help. They just want to charge up their life force energy off you. This may sound harsh for some; I know if you are wired this way you connect, and it is in your healer nature to want to help everyone. Some people are just not going to accept your help, no matter what.

We are all born with a purpose in life and lessons that our soul came here to learn. We must step into the reality of what is being shown to us. Just because we can see the soul energy of a person and what they can become it does not mean in this reality that they are choosing that path. That is one thing that we are all gifted with; free will to choose our paths. God blessed us with this. Again, it goes back full circle to the two wolves story. It can make us sad that people we care about or feel connected to make choices that hurt them. We must remember it is their choice after all and they will feel all the consequences from those choices in the end. We can only do our best to be of service if they are willing to do the work. This does not mean you will not feel the pain, for without sorrow we would not know joy.

There was one prophet in history that took on all the pain and sin of the world so you would not have to. Look what they did to Jesus Christ. He took that pain so you and

I do not have to. Our reality is forever changing. We can get off course wanting to believe that certain things are not there and get upset when we realize they are not what we wanted to see. Get back into the body and live the life you have. You may feel like you took a step back, yet you really took a step into life. I am saying you should allow yourself to be grounded without blocking your imagination. You need both in your life for balance. We all need to dream a little, play and give thanks for our many blessings.

As I end this chapter, I would like to remind you that everything energetically will have an effect on your vibration. It is your choice on whether you choose chaos or peace. Give yourself permission to step away from negative energy and watch your life change. You will be amazed when your energy shifts, at the new people that will appear in your life for the better. Be Brave, be bold and speak your truth.

## Chapter 12

## We are all Connected

*Our Father, our God, in my own consciousness let me find happiness in the love of Thee, for the love I bear toward my fellow man, Let my life, my words, my deeds, bring the joy and the happiness of the lord in Jesus to each I met day by day.*

*Edgar Cayce Reading 262-106*

Before I began writing this book the one word that rang in my head was "Freedom." I have had this in my head for many years. Little did I realize at that time it was literally for the world. My intention from the time I knew I was going to write this book was to help others who are gifted to come out from hiding. We are going to need an army of healers to help those who are wounded from all the lies, deceit, and slavery. Those who have been fearful of their connections, and being able to speak of it without ridicule, judgement, or alienation are rising to help.

We are all human beings, regardless of our skin color, we all are put together the same way for survival. Sadly though, it is our upbringing that sets us apart. It is our beliefs and the traditions of our cultures that instill what we know as the truth. I have been so blessed to have traveled and immersed myself and my children in other countries and cultures. This is what makes life magical. Embracing others and learning about their culture is a learning of life lessons. This will either make you appreciate where you came from or ignite the passion to learn more. I have felt and experienced both. For those of you who have traveled you may understand what I am talking about here.

Even though we come from different places, we are all still human beings needing all the necessities to sustain life force here on earth. That alone tells us that we are all connected. The need to step out of Ego to understand and learn this is a skill that many seem to have not learned, sad to say. Love is the only thing we take with us when our physical bodies leave this planet and spirit returns home.

As we enter the age of Aquarius you will begin to see the emergence of more lightworkers and healers enter the scene. This will be a global healing of epic proportions. This December 21, 2020, on the solstice, we step into Christ consciousness. All of those who have been led astray by the negative energies will begin a clearing, or a karmic realignment from all the evil that has been in power and has hurt the people globally. The people will rise for freedom. We are seeing it now with marches across the globe. We are rising against those who want to enslave us, by using the very thing they think can divide us, and that is our race. It will not work this time. We have risen above that vibration and are at a new level.

I had just moved to Japan from Italy. Now, if you know anything about the Italian culture it is intense and passionate. They hug, kiss, and yell a lot when they are upset. The Japanese are just the opposite. So, you can imagine how my soon to be Japanese staff was about to be taken by surprise at my (Italian) management style. It took time and adjustments on both sides, but I can say that, before I left, we were all hugging, laughing, and learning from each other. They had a new boss from the US who just left Italy with three years of learning and managing "the Italian ways." Once I settled in and took charge of the operation, I realized things here were run very differently. This company, and the way they ran it, was very calm, cool, and quiet. So much so that I felt like I was dying a slow death. I soon realized that I was brought in to shake it up and bring life back to the facility.

Being a geopathic empath, little did I know at that time that I was not only there to shake up the business, Japan would literally shake me! I would literally feel the ground rumblings beneath my feet, and I would say "did you feel that?"They would always answer 'feel what?" They were so accustomed to the Earth shifts happening there, that it was normal to them. That is unless it was a big shake. I learned so much from them as they did from me. The love and friendship that my children and I experienced there I will never forget. I am so thankful and blessed to have had the opportunity and experience. I even had a Japanese monk who lived behind me. When I first moved in, my landlord said, "please take care of my monk." I would bring him cherry pies, his favorite, and Crown Royal whiskey, another favorite of his. I do have concern for the people of Japan. They have received so many radiation hits between the atomic bomb and the 2011 earthquake it's just so sad for me to imagine today. I find it sickening that we have all this climate talk going on and no one is stepping up to help them with the radiation that is being dumped into our oceans and has been doing so for the past nine years.

Very soon, those who have been in power will begin to feel the will of the people, and the passion that freedom brings in this next decade. Aquarius is about freedom and humanity. The heavens have sent in an army of earth angels to guide us. The almighty has also opened the windows of heaven to ignite the lightworkers and healers to assist with the fallout and the planet. Because we are all connected, it is possible to send all that love to the healing of our world by being conscious of the intention to want peace, health, love, and serenity. When you think of the word "freedom" it is actually the uncovering of what has always been there. We just need to step into it, collectively knowing that nothing external is controlling us. We have this illusion that we have no free will. We all have been gifted with free will to choose. So, as a group, we can connect, come together as one and step out of the illusion that we have no control over our lives or destinies. We are also stepping into integrity. This forces us to look for truths. No matter how hard it may be to face these truths, we must, in order to shift our world to be a better place. Only with truth can we face our reality and make positive resolutions for a better world. Integrity calls for respect for yourself and others while speaking your truths. This is what I search for in a teacher, mentor, or coach. A person who has integrity. With a world full of pretenders, it can be a chore. If you step into your truth and feel the vibration of the person your gut will tell you all you need to know if you pay attention. There is a saying "if it feels or sounds too good to be true" it needs further investigation because it usually is.

Our world has been thrown into sadness. Without the darkness we do not appreciate the light. It is through our sadness and our sorrows that we can rise to have great joy. The problem is many of us get stuck in that sadness. It can freeze us if we let it, or it can free us to create change. Our sadness links us to the great pain felt in our hearts. Have you ever noticed someone sad, having a bad day, only later to find out that they suffered a huge life blow? You may have thought to yourself that you could have been nicer to that person. We have all done that from time to time without realizing, because we were in our own sadness. We were unable to see the pain in others. I encourage those of you who are now reading this to realize this and become aware that we are all human. And at some point, in all of our lives, we have suffered a heart break that has hit us at our core. Some of us choose to put it aside because we feel it is too painful to deal with. I encourage you to cry it out if you need to or can, and work on getting that sadness and broken heart energy out. Masking, hiding or ignoring these emotions will only hold your spiritual growth back, and it will surface in other ways in your life without you even being aware it is happening. Only after facing it can you heal and grow. We then become a beacon for others to follow.

In this work, that I have been doing now for years, I have found that the most gifted compassionate people are those who have suffered so much. They appreciate every blessing that comes into their lives and choose to not be labeled as a victim. I am always amazed at how we run into people that we have not seen in years from far corners of the earth and it lets us know that the world can be a small place. When we all come together in unity, which I know we will, the positive changes will emerge as we enter this new age.

Now, I want you to think about what kind of connections you would like to make in your life right now. No matter what it is, start praying for it, asking your angels and guides to assist you with this, and write it down. They long for us to ask for their help, and they delight in assisting. Whenever I have found myself wanting to learn something, the teacher appears. I must say that it is quite magical. Instead of going against the grain, go with the grain of life. There is a saying that *a tree that bends withstands the storms, the stiff and rigid ones break.* Believe it or not, our bodies and minds intuitively know how to survive, and we are all connected that way. If forced to, we would adapt for survival. I am going to make a prediction here that the information about area 51 will be released soon. We are not the only intelligent beings in our solar system, although they may be thinking the way we are behaving is not highly intelligent. I have had clients come to me for hypnosis for alien abduction experiences. I have even had other mediums say the angelic light beings I have seen are aliens. What do you say to this? Do you believe in other forms of life outside of earth?

    I love listening to the Edgar Cayce readings of Atlantis. You may find those readings very intriguing as well. I feel we are in a time remarkably similar with today's event. According to these readings, Atlantis failed because they went away from the soul. They were very advanced in technology for their time. We are in a very spiritual time of awakening right now. This Christmas will be aligned with Christ consciousness. Even though you may be apprehensive, I encourage you to seek your own growth, I have always been drawn to spirituality and things unseen, in the shadows.

    My intention with this book and the storytelling is let

you know that you are not alone, and there are others like you. Being in service and helping others has always been second nature to me. I had to learn the hard way that being too nice can get you taken advantage of if you do not set those personal boundaries. The key is to be able to help others so they can get past whatever issues that they need help with and move on to a better place. Some will try their darndest to become dependent on you, so be very careful of this. I have a friend who is a medium that never learned how to say "no." People would call this poor woman all hours of the night. When she got married her husband put a stop to the boundary breakers. He let them know that although his wife is gifted, she is also a human being. People that we are really connected to and understand us seem to just step into protecting our best interests by having our backs instinctively.

Doing this work is more than just talking, like some people may think. Taking on other people's energy is exhausting. And doing the medium work is a whole other level of raising the vibration for connection. Those that have no idea of how this works, why this works and who want to analyze everything, are lost to the experiences of the magic, mystery and miracles life has to offer.

The empaths, intuitive, and mediums of the world are very much like the canaries that go down into the coal mines. They alert us. When seeking psychic help, I encourage you to do a little homework first. Like every occupation on the planet, there are bad apples in this vocation as well. This chapter is about connections. I find that when I am looking for a certain thing, it always shows at the right time. The morale of this whole story is that the universe puts us in the places we need to be, at the proper time in our lives. Whether it is the loss of a job, spouse, mate, family member or home, believe that when one door closes another will open. What would our lives be without our lessons? By helping others heal, release pain, fears, phobias etc., we create a ripple effect of universal love. We step into creating a reality that we were born to step into.

With common affinity, linkage, and relationship to humanity, we can choose collectively to become a liaison for a better world. The soulless digital, disconnected world of today will see much humility and what kind of damage to the human spirit, and crimes against humanity, it has caused. 2020 is, and was, a spiritual war for humanity. 2020 is linked to clear vision, the veil has been lifted and the truths are all coming forward.

Will you let go of all preconceived illusions and ego? God is ultimately in charge. No matter what direction we decide to choose, he gives us the ability to choose a path and with each path there will be a result. Sometimes the easy one ends up being the hardest and most brutal one. Step out of your comfort zone to new possibilities with love, faith, and humanity. Think peace, love, unity, harmony and radiate that energy and those thoughts out to everyone you meet. Let us all collectively raise the vibration of the planet, leaving the ego, evil and greed of the past to fall. No one else oversees your thoughts and actions. Being a victim keeps you in a mind prison that is just an illusion. Now is the time to step up and become a truth and love warrior. May your journey into the age of Aquarius and Christ consciousness be blessed with health, love, and prosperity.

# ABOUT THE AUTHOR

Gail Webster Cht. has been intuitive all her life. Born and raised in New England. A professional Intuitive who has given thousands of readings to clients from all over the world and all walks of life. What was once a hobby and study turned into a career of change agent, grief healer, hypnotherapist, comedy stage hypnotist, medium, author, aspiring mentalist that she is today. The gift of intuition and empathy only enhances the tools that she uses to help others make positive changes in their lives for the better. Helping people whether it is through readings, hypnosis, coaching or laughter at her comedy stage shows. Certified in past life regressions, lives in between lives and future lives. She uses her intuition in all her services as she did when she was employed by the Department of Defense. Traveled around the world and met so many souls from all walks of life. Learned from life's experiences and some wonderful teachers. A graduate of the school of hard knocks with honors. Born to make a difference in this lifetime and believes those that are brought to read this book about the gift sprinkled with its real-life stories are too. There are so many people needing healers, coaches, and therapists in their lives. I hope you will gain insight through this book that you too can make a difference with your gifts and purpose in this world. Currently living in the State of Maine with her two Siamese cats Merlin & Aphrodite. Soon she will be on a new adventure south.

# Resources

You Can Heal Your Life by Louise L Hay

The Power of Intention by Dr. Wayne W. Dyer

Trust Your Vibes by Sonia Choquette

The Disappearance of the Universe by Gary R. Renard

Practical Law of Attraction by Victoria M. Gallagher

Born Knowing by John Holland

Denial Is Not A River In Egypt by Shelly Stockwell, PH. D

The Self-Hypnosis Solution by Dr. Richard K Nongard

Bridging Two Realms by John Holland

Where Two Worlds Meet by Janet Nohavec with Suzanne Giesemann

Animal Spirit Guides by Steven D. Farmer, PH.D.

Animal Speak by Ted Andrews

A Course in Miracles by Helen Schucman

Archangels & Ascended Masters by Doreen Virtue PH.D.

Ask and It Is Given by Ester and Jerry Hicks (The Teachings of Abraham)

The Secret by Rhonda Byrne

The Four Agreements by Don Miguel Ruiz with Janet Mills.

These are just some of the many resources and books. What is so wonderful about empaths they can walk into a bookstore and just put their hand on a book that they need to read. No, you may gaze at an Amazon list and pick what you gravitate to.

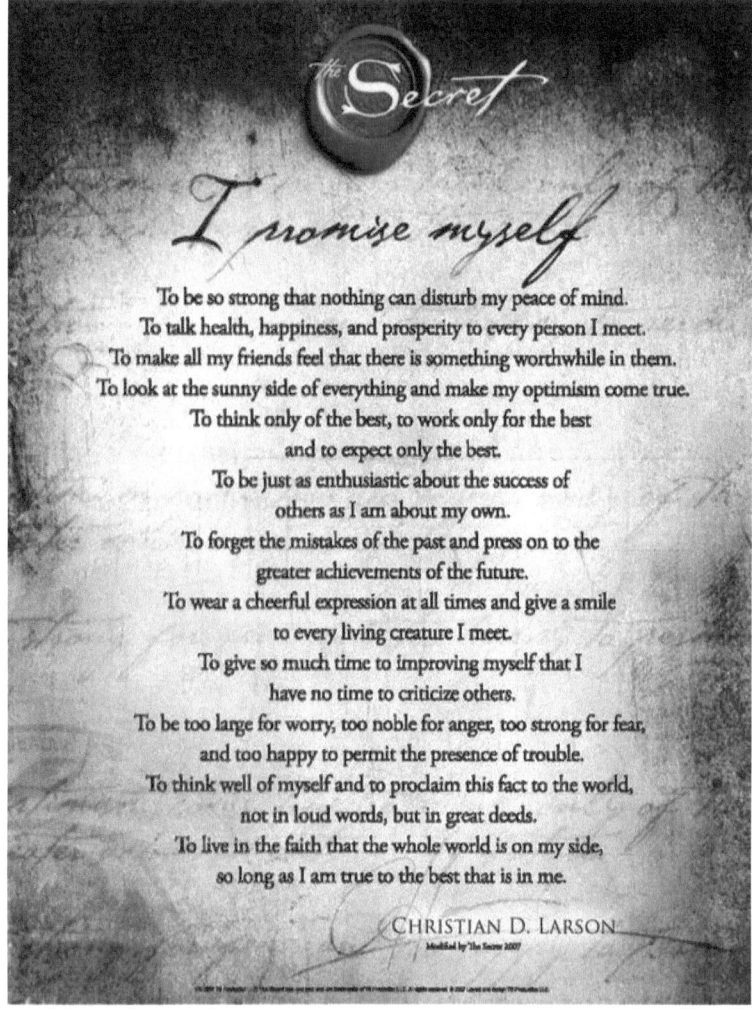

www.ingramcontent.com/pod-product-compliance
Lightning Source LLC
Chambersburg PA
CBHW020911080526
44589CB00011B/544